FAST FEASTS

FAST FEASTS

QUICK, EASY RECIPES WITH A MIDDLE EASTERN TWIST

John Gregory-Smith

OH EDITIONS

CONTENTS

INTRODUCTION

If the last few years have taught me anything, it's that the power of food is more important than ever. During the height of the COVID-19 pandemic, when we were first told to stay at home and not go near our loved ones, many of us went back to basics – and food was the greatest crutch: an indulgence, a distraction (hands up who cooked sourdough?) and a connection to those we couldn't sit and eat with.

Food became a hot topic of conversation, up there with the latest Netflix series and what home workout was in vogue. As the world opened up, hopping around to a 30-minute body attack on YouTube or marvelling at the Tiger King's mullet seems like a lifetime away. But food is still on the table. It's an utter joy being in a restaurant and hearing the roar of service and the chatter of content diners. Having people over for a meal is everything. Getting to sit and laugh with your nearest and dearest over a bowl of something delish is an elixir. In fact, I don't think I will ever take such a simple pleasure for granted again.

Like so many of you, my career changed in 2020. I have always travelled extensively for work, exploring the Middle East and feeding my infatuation for the rich cuisine of this region. From a very young age, this part of the world tickled my taste buds and has become my specialty as a chef. I take pride in pushing myself to go off the beaten track to discover new dishes to share with you guys. My last trip in

2019 was to Gaza with World Food Programme, an extraordinary charity that feeds millions across the globe. Here I discovered a type of Arabic food I had not seen before – one that relishes spicy heat (you don't often see chillies used in Arabic cooking). It was extraordinary. I came back buzzing and planned to write a book detailing what I had found. But just like that, in the blink of an eye, everything changed. There was no travel, no book and I couldn't see a way to continue the niche I had carved out.

I'm very ambitious and, coupled with an extraordinary amount of energy, it was hard not to have a project to focus on or a new goal to achieve. If I am honest, I felt hopeless. It was very odd. But like so many times in my life, the kitchen called me back. During lockdown I went to live with my family and allocated myself the job of official house chef. I went back to basics, making what they wanted or inventing new dishes using ingredients we already had in the kitchen.

As life unfolded, I was able to get more creative. I felt confident leaning on the knowledge I had honed over so many years, and began throwing the flavours of the Middle East into the everyday dishes I was preparing. Suddenly, I was the king of spicy traybakes and easy one-pots. I even found myself using ingredients that I had not touched for years. I fell back in love with jacket potatoes. They have always reminded me of my old school dinners, laden with unbranded baked beans and hard cheese. I hadn't had one for years. But, hello, cooked well with a few things I like and suddenly you're talking.

I've always been uneasy writing recipes from places I've not been to. In fact, during my career, I have made a furious point of going everywhere to experience the cuisine first-hand before talking about it. But the rug was pulled from under me and I couldn't get inspiration from travelling. When I felt stale and needed a refresh, I did the unthinkable and from my living room travelled to pastures new. I toured Iran, Iraq and Afghanistan, reading about dishes I never knew existed. I threw these ideas into recipes I was working on, mashing things up to create something fresh and exciting. I was happy again; feeding the family had sorted me out. At the same time, this new style of cookery reignited my career that I had all but forgotten: I began sharing recipe videos on my social channels, documenting my dishes and you guys lapped them up. What started as something to keep me busy is now a full-time job. Not only have I written this book but I produce and share new content on my social channels every week, have a *Telegraph* column and I'm regularly cooking up a storm on TV. It's funny how things fall into place when you least expect them to.

Fast Feasts is a celebration of the bond we all have with food. It's a collection of recipes that I have been cooking for my friends and family over the last few years. Some are twists on classic dishes that you will know and others are paired-back versions of something incredible I picked up on my travels. It's also an insistence that every meal should be a cracker. I'm no fool and well aware that for this to work, especially when everyone's lives are getting busier, cooking has to be easy and taste bloody great. And you know what? I promise you, it can. In this book, I cover everything from speedy Monday night meals when you don't have the energy to do anything, to simple working-from-home lunches,

"GETTING TO SIT AND LAUGH WITH YOUR NEAREST AND DEAREST OVER A BOWL OF SOMETHING DELISH IS AN ELIXIR. IN FACT, I DON'T THINK I WILL EVER TAKE SUCH A SIMPLE PLEASURE FOR GRANTED AGAIN."

killer comfort food to enjoy on the sofa and effortless entertaining.

If you follow me on social media, you'll know that I get extreme pleasure from food. I inadvertently dance when I'm working in the kitchen and if I really like the taste of something, I jump up and down like a small child. Cooking should be fun, especially if you are cooking for others. There is nothing worse than working yourself into a lather when you have people coming over. It should be a doddle so you can enjoy the company of those you invited. The recipes in *Fast Feasts* are all stripped back and simple, relying on big flavours to do all the work. I have included my Storecupboard Staples on pages 10–11 so you can see what to stock up on. If you want more inspiration to cook for a crowd, I've put together some dinner party combos on pages 182–83. They are all do ahead kind of dinners so you have more time to glam up and appreciate the party as much as everyone else.

Fast Feasts was inspired by you and is for you. Thanks for sticking with me. ◆

STORECUPBOARD STAPLES

BAHARAT

An epic blend of spices found all over the Middle East, with a lovely woody aroma that smells of Christmas. It's fantastic for injecting a background warmth to marinades and casseroles.

DRIED HERBS

These add a different dimension to fresh herbs, and generally have a mellower tone so you can add them at the beginning of the cooking process. Oregano literally smells like spring in the Levant and dried mint is more spearmint than its fresh counterpart.

DUKKAH

Originally from Egypt, this incredible mix is a blend of herbs, spices and nuts that makes a sensational seasoning to use on any roasted meats or to add texture to a traybake.

PESTO

The green kind with its sweet basil fragrance and the red kind with an umami hit from the sun-dried tomatoes, flavour anything from plain pasta to a cheese toasty or even a bowl of soup. Find a brand you like and make sure you always have them in the cupboard.

POMEGRANATE MOLASSES

Made by cooking and reducing pomegranate juice, this sweet-sour sticky molasses is an instant win for salads and great as an alternative to lemon juice in stews and soups. Make sure you find one with a high percentage of pomegranate in the ingredients.

NUTS

I have a whole cupboard full of nuts – almonds, pistachios, walnuts, cashew nuts and pine nuts – that I use to garnish so many different dishes. I buy them toasted where I can but if not, dry-fry them in a frying pan (skillet), shaking regularly for a few minutes over a lowish heat until golden.

PRESERVED LEMONS

A staple of Moroccan cooking, these are fresh lemons that have been preserved in salt. Over time, this mellows the tart tang into something wonderfully fragrant. You can add them to tagines for a subtle note or chop them into salad dressings for a more intense experience.

ROSE HARISSA

Made from dried chillies, caraway and rose water, this North African spice paste is incredible to add a hit of heat to anything you fancy. You can use it as a condiment or bung it into a soup or stew during the cooking process. It also pairs unbelievably well with hummus.

ROSE WATER

This incredible perfumed water is so evocative of the Middle East, where it's a key component in many sweet dishes. The clear liquid adds a subtle floral tone that you can add to bakes and cheesecakes.

SMOKED PAPRIKA

This little spice really packs a punch, with its bright red colour and wonderfully smoky flavour. You can find different varieties, sweet or spicy. It's great if you want a barbecue vibe when you're cooking inside.

SRIRACHA

The ultimate chilli sauce, with a lovely sharp heat and full-on fruity tang. It's a South-East Asian condiment but frankly works magically on everything.

SPICES

I have kept the list of spices to a minimum for this book, choosing key spices that add masses of flavour: cumin, coriander, fenugreek, ground ginger, chilli flakes, allspice, turmeric and sumac.

TAHINI

This glossy paste is made from ground sesame seeds and has an intense nutty flavour. The natural oils make it very rich and feel really indulgent. It's the key ingredient in hummus but you can use it in so many different ways, from drizzling over salads to swirling on top of brownies.

TURKISH PEPPER FLAKES

Also known as Aleppo pepper flakes or *pul biber*, these are beautifully smoked vibrant red pepper flakes. They impart a mild heat and smokiness to anything. If you swirl them into melted butter, they glow like the sunset and you can drizzle this over pasta, kebabs or stews to add bucketloads of flavour.

SALT & PEPPER

It may look bizarre referencing these guys but they are key ingredients in most things. For salt, I always use Maldon salt flakes. I love the texture and taste – it brings out the flavour of whatever you are cooking. I tend to use freshly ground black pepper as a spice and less of a seasoning, although a pinch of pepper is an easy win to anything savoury.

ZA'ATAR

One of the main flavours of Lebanon, this spice mix is made from dried herbs – normally oregano or thyme – as well as sumac (a tart red berry that's ground to a powder) and toasted sesame seeds. It's sour, aromatic and nutty. You can rain za'atar down onto most things, from salads to roast lamb, or try pairing it with creamy sauces or melted cheese. ◆

EVERYDAY

EASY

▼

SOME OF MY BEST-KEPT SECRETS ARE IN THIS
CHAPTER – WELL, THE CULINARY ONES ANYWAY.
THESE ARE THE RECIPES THAT I MAKE TIME AND TIME
AGAIN DURING THE WEEK WHEN I GET IN LATE AND
DON'T FEEL LIKE COOKING ANYTHING. I'M TALKING
QUICK-PREP, SPEEDY MID-WEEK LIFESAVERS.

WHEN I NEED SOMETHING FROM FRIDGE TO FORK
FAST, I STILL WANT FLAVOURS THAT EXCITE ME, AND
BIG FLAVOURS ARE THE KEY TO SUCCESS HERE. I
HAVE GONE EASY ON INGREDIENTS, CHOOSING ONLY
THE LOUDEST ONES, SO YOU CAN RUSTLE UP ANY OF
THESE RECIPES IN UNDER 30 MINUTES.

STEAK TAGLIATA WITH ZHOUG

SERVES

2

You really don't get a speedier supper than steak tagliata, an iconic Italian salad of thinly sliced steak, peppery rocket and shaved Parmesan. My version sticks to the original but with the addition of a tangy zhoug dressing. Zhoug is a Yemenite salsa made with herbs, chillies and spices. I like mine sharp, but if you want it sweeter, add a teaspoon of caster sugar.

For the zhoug

- 1 garlic clove
- 1 green chilli, deseeded if you like, roughly chopped
- 2 tsp ground cumin
- a large handful of roughly chopped parsley leaves
- a large handful of roughly chopped coriander (cilantro) leaves and stalks
- 2 tbsp white wine vinegar
- 1 tbsp olive oil
- 1 tbsp water
- sea salt

For the salad

- 1 tsp olive oil
- 2 sirloin steaks (about 200g/7oz each), at room temperature
- 70g (2¼oz) rocket (arugula)
- Parmesan shavings, to serve

Method

1. Start by making the zhoug. Chuck all the zhoug ingredients into a mini chopper with a good pinch of salt and blitz to a smooth dressing. If it looks too thick, add another tablespoon of water and blitz again.

2. Heat a non-stick frying pan (skillet) or griddle pan over a high heat. Brush the oil over both sides of the steaks and season with plenty of salt. Cook for 2 minutes on each side until golden. I love rare steak, so I take them out here. If you want medium rare, reduce the heat to low and cook for another 1 minute on each side. Either way, rest the steaks on a plate, covered with kitchen foil, for 5 minutes.

3. Tip the rocket into a mixing bowl, add 2 tablespoons of the zhoug and toss together. Divide between two serving plates.

4. Slice up the steaks, removing the fat, and place over the salad. Top each plate with the remaining zhoug and the resting juices. Serve immediately with the Parmesan scattered over the top.

THE ULTIMATE FISH FINGER SARNIE

SERVES

4

One of my best friends always laughs at me for making fish finger sandwiches. He feels that they are not worthy of a recipe. Boo to that, I say – they are one of the most delicious things to eat. My mayonnaise is incredibly savoury with sun-dried tomatoes and pomegranate molasses and, you know what, together they make the most divine dinner when you can't be bothered to cook.

Ingredients

+ 2 tbsp olive oil
+ 16 fish fingers
+ 50g (1¾oz) sun-dried tomatoes in oil, drained
+ 2 tsp Turkish pepper flakes
+ 1 tsp pomegranate molasses
+ 100g (3½oz/scant ½ cup) mayonnaise
+ 8 slices of bread of your choice
+ 1 baby gem (bibb) lettuce, picked
+ sea salt and freshly ground black pepper
+ hot sauce, to serve (I love Franks)

Method

1. Heat the oil in a large non-stick frying pan (skillet) over a medium heat and cook the fish fingers for 8–10 minutes, turning every 2–3 minutes until cooked through and golden.

2. Meanwhile, chuck the sun-dried tomatoes, Turkish pepper flakes and pomegranate molasses into a mini chopper and blitz until smooth. Tip into a bowl and add the mayonnaise. Mix well then season to taste.

3. Slather the mayonnaise onto four slices of the bread and top each with four fish fingers. Place the lettuce and then the remaining bread on top and serve immediately with hot sauce at the table.

AFGHAN CHICKEN CURRY

SERVES

4

This is my version of a very quick and easy Afghan curry called *lavand-e-murgh* or chicken in yogurt. The main flavour comes from baharat, a classic Middle Eastern blend made of woody spices – think coriander, cloves and black pepper. Once the chicken is cooked and the sauce reduced, you add the yogurt. This keeps it from splitting and makes the sauce even creamier, so you need full-fat yogurt for this to work.

Ingredients

* 1 onion, roughly chopped
* 1 green chilli, deseeded if you like, roughly chopped
* 4 garlic cloves
* 2.5cm (1in) ginger root, peeled and roughly chopped
* 2 tbsp olive oil
* 2 cardamom pods, crushed
* 2 tsp baharat
* 600g (1lb 5oz) boneless, skinless chicken thigh fillets, cut into bite-sized pieces
* juice of ½ lime
* 150g (5oz/⅔ cup) Greek yogurt
* sea salt
* handful of finely chopped coriander (cilantro) leaves
* boiled rice, to serve

Method

1. Put the onion, chilli, garlic and ginger into a mini chopper and pulse until fine. Feel free to finely chop by hand, if you like.

2. Heat the oil in a wok over a medium heat. Add the cardamom, the onion mixture and a pinch of salt and mix well. Cook, stirring occasionally, for 6–8 minutes until the onions are lovely and soft.

3. Add the baharat, chicken and a little more salt. Mix well. Pour in 250ml (8½fl oz/1 cup) of just-boiled water, which should nearly cover the chicken. Turn up the heat and bring to the boil. Reduce the heat to a simmer and cook, stirring occasionally, for 10 minutes. Increase the heat to medium–high so it's bubbling away, then cook, stirring occasionally, for 10 minutes until the chicken is cooked through and the sauce reduced by half.

4. Take the pan off the heat and add the lime juice and yogurt. Stir together and check the seasoning, adding salt to taste. Scatter over the coriander and serve immediately with rice.

CREAMY CHICKEN PASTA

SERVES

4

This incredible chicken pasta recipe was inspired by a dish from the North Caucasus called Chicken *Circassian*, a salad with a thick sauce made from ground walnuts and spices. It's almost like Coronation chicken. I love using walnuts to thicken the sauce. They add bucketloads of flavour. You want to grind them really fine, almost to a paste, before you add them to the chicken.

Top Tip

Defrost fully before reheating and then add a splash of water to get the sauce lovely and creamy again.

Ingredients

- 2 tbsp olive oil
- 1 onion, roughly chopped
- 400g (14oz/1½ cups) orecchiette
- 400g (14oz) chicken breasts, cut into 2.5cm (1in) chunks
- 2 garlic cloves, crushed
- 50g (1¾oz/½ cup) walnuts, blended until fine
- 1 tbsp tomato purée (paste)
- 2 tsp smoked paprika
- 2 tsp paprika
- 120ml (4fl oz/½ cup) sour cream
- a large handful of finely chopped tarragon leaves
- sea salt and freshly ground black pepper
- Parmesan, to serve

Method

1. Heat the oil in a large non-stick pan over a medium heat. Add the onion and cook, stirring occasionally, for 6–8 minutes until golden.

2. Cook the orecchiette in boiling salted water for 8–10 minutes, or according to the packet instructions, until al dente. Drain and set to one side.

3. Add the chicken and garlic to the pan with the onion and mix well. Cook for 2–3 minutes, stirring occasionally, to get some heat into the chicken. Add the walnuts, tomato purée, smoked paprika, paprika, a good pinch of salt and pepper and 200ml (7fl oz/scant 1 cup) of just-boiled water. Mix well and bring to the boil. Cover, reduce the heat to low and cook for 6–8 minutes or until the chicken is just cooked through and tender.

4. Chuck the cooked pasta into the pan with the chicken. Turn the heat up to medium and bubble away for 1–2 minutes, stirring occasionally, until the sauce clings to the pasta. Add the sour cream and tarragon, mix well and serve immediately with plenty of Parmesan.

PORK CHOPS AND
BUTTER BEAN MASH

SERVES

4

To give these pork chops maximum flavour, I use a marinading technique that I picked up on a research trip to Ramallah in the West Bank of Palestine. The base is mayonnaise and it's mixed with lemon, tomato purée and spices. The mayo helps tenderise the meat and caramelises beautifully when cooked.

Top Tip

This recipe works beautifully with lamb chops. The cooking time is the same.

Ingredients

- 50g (1¾oz/¼ cup) mayonnaise
- juice of ½ lemon
- 2 tsp tomato purée (paste)
- 1 tsp Turkish pepper flakes
- 1 tsp ground black pepper
- 4 pork chops (250g/9oz each)
- 1 tbsp olive oil
- 1 garlic clove, thinly sliced
- 2 x 400g (14oz) tins of butter beans, drained
- 1 tsp ground cumin
- sea salt and freshly ground black pepper
- rocket (arugula), to serve

Method

1. Preheat the grill to high. Put the mayonnaise, half the lemon juice, the tomato purée, Turkish pepper flakes, black pepper and a good pinch of salt into a mixing bowl. Mix well. Add the chops and rub the marinade all over them. Place onto a grill rack and grill for 3–4 minutes each side until charred and tender.

2. Meanwhile, heat the oil in a saucepan over a medium heat and add the garlic. Cook, stirring occasionally, for 30–60 seconds until fragrant. Tip in the beans and 70ml (about 5 tablespoons) of just-boiled water. Add the cumin and plenty of salt and pepper. Mash together. You can go as smooth as you like. I like creamy with a little texture. If the beans look too dry, add a little more water – 2–4 teaspoons should do it.

3. To serve, divide the mash between four plates and top each one with a chop. I like to add a little salt to the meat at this stage. Serve immediately with a handful of rocket.

VEGGIE SHAKSHUKA

SERVES

4

A shakshuka is a staple for me. I love it for brunch and as a quick mid-week meal. I developed this vegetarian version for the mighty actor Lena Headey, aka Cersei Lannister, for a charity cook-off we did together. If you want to save time on the chopping, chuck the tomatoes into a food processor to break them down.

Top Tip

Add chopped chorizo to the onions and pepper for a different spin.

Ingredients

- 2 tbsp olive oil
- 1 red onion, finely chopped
- 1 red (bell) pepper, finely chopped
- 2 garlic cloves, finely chopped
- 4 tomatoes, finely chopped
- 1 tbsp tomato purée (paste)
- 2 tsp smoked paprika
- 1 tsp chilli (hot pepper) flakes
- ½ x 400g tin of chickpeas (garbanzos) (about 100g/3½oz drained weight), drained and rinsed
- 4 eggs
- A small handful of roughly chopped parsley leaves
- 2 tbsp tahini
- sea salt
- bread, to serve

Method

1. Heat the oil in a large non-stick frying pan (skillet) over a medium heat. Add the onion and pepper and cook, stirring occasionally, for 6–8 minutes until a little golden.

2. Add the garlic, tomatoes, tomato purée, smoked paprika, chilli flakes, a good pinch of salt and 2 tablespoons of water. Turn the heat up a little and mix well. Cook, stirring occasionally, for 6–8 minutes until the tomatoes have broken down into a thick sauce. If it gets too dry, add a little water to help. Tip in the chickpeas and mix well.

3. Using the back of a spoon, make 4 wells in the sauce and crack the eggs into them. Season the whites with salt and cook for 5–6 minutes. To help the whites set and keep the yolks runny, muddle the whites into the sauce with a teaspoon every few minutes.

4. Scatter the parsley over the top of your shakshuka and drizzle over the tahini. Serve immediately with plenty of bread.

COCONUT HARISSA MEATBALLS

SERVES
4

This meatball stew is a true JGS invention. It uses two of my favourite ingredients, coconut milk and rose harissa, creating a spicy sauce in seconds. The flavours work so well together, and I love this with brown rice. Now, I have not gone all worthy on you, I just think in this instance the nuttiness works so well with the other flavours. Feel free to use white basmati if you like. After all, it's your dinner.

Top Tip
For a leaner version, use turkey mince instead of lamb.

Ingredients

- 600g (1lb 5oz) lean minced (ground) lamb
- 2 tbsp olive oil
- 1 onion, finely chopped
- 2 garlic cloves, crushed
- 3 tbsp rose harissa
- 1 x 400ml (13fl oz) tin of coconut milk
- juice of ¼ lemon
- a small handful of coriander (cilantro) leaves
- sea salt
- boiled rice, to serve

Method

1. Put the lamb into a mixing bowl with plenty of salt. Roll into 24 walnut-sized meatballs.

2. Heat the oil in a large non-stick frying pan (skillet) and add the meatballs. Cook for 2–3 minutes on two sides until a little golden. Remove from the pan and set to one side.

3. Chuck the onion into the same pan and cook, stirring occasionally, for 4–5 minutes until golden. Watch the heat so it does not burn. Add the garlic and cook, stirring occasionally, for 30 seconds until fragrant. Add the harissa, coconut milk, lemon juice and a pinch of salt. Mix well and bring to the boil.

4. Return the meatballs to the sauce. Cover, reduce the heat to low and cook for 6–8 minutes until just cooked through.

5. Remove the lid, increase the heat to medium and let it bubble away for 4–5 minutes until the sauce is really thick. Remember to keep basting and turning the meatballs, so they stay super-juicy. Some brands of rose harissa can be fairly oily, so I like to skim off the excess fat once the sauce has reduced. Sprinkle with coriander and serve immediately with rice.

SALMON TRAYBAKE WITH PEA AND FETA MASH

SERVES

4

A salmon traybake is a mid-week staple that most of us have ready to rock in our repertoire, and my version is a must-try. It couldn't be simpler. The salmon is cooked with cherry tomatoes and then served with a pea and feta mash. The salty cheese and sweet peas go together like old friends.

Ingredients

- 4 salmon fillets, skin on if you like
- 200g (7oz) cherry tomatoes
- 2 tbsp olive oil, plus extra for drizzling
- 600g (1lb 5oz/scant 4 cups) frozen peas
- 160g (5½oz) feta
- juice of 2 lemons
- sea salt
- chilli (hot pepper) flakes (optional), to serve

Method

1. Preheat the oven to 180°C fan (350°F/gas 6). Put the salmon and cherry tomatoes into a roasting dish and pour over the oil. Add a good pinch of salt and mix well. Roast for 20–25 minutes, or until the salmon is just cooked through.

2. Meanwhile, cook the peas for 2–3 minutes in a saucepan of boiling water. Drain, give a little rinse under the cold tap and drain again.

3. Tip the peas into a food processor and add the feta, lemon juice and a pinch of salt. Blitz to a coarse mixture.

4. To serve, divide the mash between four serving plates and top each one with salmon and tomatoes. Drizzle over a little olive oil and serve with a pinch of chilli flakes, if you like the extra heat.

CREAMY HARISSA GNOCCHI

SERVES
4

When hunger strikes and you need something to eat fast, my Creamy Harissa Gnocchi is just the ticket. It goes from fridge to fork in 15 minutes. I use shop-bought gnocchi and boil it until pillowy soft, then pan-fry a small batch for texture. Cream cheese and harissa melt together to make a speedy sauce. It's incredibly comforting. I love to eat this on a Monday night after a long weekend.

Ingredients

- 1kg (2lb 4 oz) fresh gnocchi
- 40g (1½oz) butter
- 100g (3½oz) cream cheese
- 2 tbsp rose harissa
- a large handful of finely chopped chives
- sea salt
- grated Parmesan, to serve

Method

1. Cook the gnocchi in a large pan of boiling salted water for 2–3 minutes, or as directed on the packet, until they float to the surface and are lovely and fluffy. Using a heatproof jug, carefully scoop out 100ml (3½fl oz/scant ½ cup) of the cooking water for the sauce and then drain the gnocchi well.

2. Melt the butter in a large non-stick pan over a medium heat. Depending on the size of your pan, add a layer of gnocchi. You don't want too much or it won't fry, so make sure there a little space around each piece. Add a pinch of salt and fry for 4–5 minutes until golden on one side.

3. Give the gnocchi in the pan a good shake and add the cream cheese, rose harissa, the remaining gnocchi and the reserved water. Mix well and cook for 1–2 minutes until the sauce clings to the gnocchi. Add most of the chives and mix well. Check the seasoning and add salt to taste.

4. Divide the gnocchi between four serving bowls and top with the remaining chives. Serve immediately scattered with grated Parmesan.

PRAWNS WITH ORZO TABBOULEH

SERVES

4

A traditional tabbouleh uses mountains of fresh herbs and a small amount of bulgur wheat. My version turns this around and uses orzo as the main ingredient, with the zingy herbs running through it. This is topped with garlicky prawns and crumbled feta to make a mouth-watering meal that's ready in minutes.

Top Tip

This is great for picnics or lunch al desko in the office as nothing wilts in your Tupperware box.

Ingredients

- 350g (12oz/4 cups) orzo
- juice of 1 lemon and zest of ½ lemon
- 1 tbsp olive oil
- 2 handfuls of finely chopped coriander (cilantro) leaves
- 2 handfuls of finely chopped parsley leaves
- 200g (7oz) cherry tomatoes, halved
- 30g (1oz) butter
- 300g (10½oz) raw peeled king prawns
- 3 garlic cloves, finely sliced
- 2 tsp Turkish pepper flakes
- 1 tsp tomato purée (paste)
- 30g (1oz) feta
- sea salt

Method

1. Cook the orzo in a pan of boiling salted water for 5–6 minutes, or according to the packet instructions, until al dente. Drain and give it a blast of cold water to stop it sticking together, then drain again thoroughly.

2. Put the cooked orzo into a mixing bowl. Add the lemon juice, olive oil, herbs, tomatoes and a good pinch of salt and mix together.

3. Melt the butter in a non-stick frying pan (skillet) over a medium–high heat. Add the prawns, garlic and a good pinch of salt. Stir-fry for 2–3 minutes, or until the prawns are just cooked. Add the Turkish pepper flakes, the lemon zest and tomato purée. Mix well and take the pan off the heat.

4. Arrange the orzo on a serving dish and top with the prawns. Drizzle over all the butter that's left in the pan – it's divine. Crumble over the feta and serve immediately.

CHARRED DUKKAH LAMB CUTLETS

SERVES

4

Lamb cutlets are one of the best express ingredients to use when you need something on the table pronto. I make a fiery crust of dukkah and chilli flakes to coat the cutlets and then chuck them under the grill to cook. In true kebab-house style, I bung the lamb onto flatbreads, which soak up the resting juices, and serve them with minty yogurt and a chunky salad.

Ingredients

- 2 tbsp dukkah
- 1–2 tsp chilli (hot pepper) flakes (2 is hot)
- 8 lamb cutlets (chops) (about 600g/1lb 5oz)
- 2 tbsp olive oil
- 2 handfuls of mint leaves
- 250g (9oz/1 cup) Greek yogurt
- juice of 1½ lemons
- 250g (9oz) cucumber, cut into 2cm (¾in) chunks
- ½ red onion, thinly sliced
- 3 tomatoes, roughly chopped
- 4 flatbreads
- sea salt

Method

1. Preheat the grill to high. Mix the dukkah with the chilli flakes and a good pinch of salt. Rub all over the lamb so it has a thick crust of spices. Brush both sides of the meat with half the olive oil and place onto a grill rack. Grill for 1–2 minutes each side until charred on the outside but still pink in the middle.

2. Meanwhile, finely chop half the mint and mix it with the yogurt, the juice of half a lemon and a good pinch of salt in a mixing bowl.

3. Roughly chop the remaining mint and chuck it in another mixing bowl with the cucumber, red onion, tomatoes, and the remaining lemon juice and olive oil. Add a pinch of salt and toss together.

4. Fold the flatbreads in half and pop the cooked lamb onto them – they will soak up the resting juices. Divide the salad and yogurt between the plates and dive in.

CAULIFLOWER RICE PILAF

SERVES

4

My Cauliflower Rice Pilaf is based on the perfectly tender pilaf dishes of the Middle East, but quicker to make and packed with vegetables – which is how I love to eat during the week. Don't worry, this doesn't mean you will be hungry two minutes later. Far from it. A tin of chickpeas bulks it up and for maximum flavour I grate over a little halloumi at the end. This melts into the cauliflower rice and adds a sophisticated saltiness.

Top Tip

Skip the grated halloumi to make this vegan.

Ingredients

- 2 tbsp olive oil
- 1 red onion, finely chopped
- 1 red (bell) pepper, finely chopped
- 2 tomatoes, finely chopped
- 450g (1lb) cauliflower florets
- 2 tbsp sun-dried tomato paste
- 2 tsp dried mint
- 1 tsp Turkish pepper flakes, plus extra for sprinkling (optional)
- ½ tsp ground black pepper
- 1 x 400g (14oz) tin of chickpeas (garbanzos), drained and rinsed
- 1 handful of finely chopped parsley leaves
- 60g (2oz) halloumi
- sea salt

Method

1. Heat the oil in a large saucepan over a medium heat and add the onion and pepper. Cook, stirring occasionally, for 6–8 minutes until the onion is golden. Add the tomatoes and a good pinch of salt. Turn the heat up a little and mix well. Cook, stirring occasionally, for 4–5 minutes until the tomatoes have broken down.

2. Meanwhile, chuck the cauliflower into a food processor and blitz into cauliflower rice. You might need to do this in 3–4 batches.

3. Add the cauliflower, sun-dried tomato paste, dried mint, Turkish pepper flakes, black pepper, chickpeas and a good pinch of salt to the pan with the onions. Pour over 150ml (5fl oz/scant ⅔ cup) of just-boiled water. Cover, reduce the heat to low and cook for 6–8 minutes until the cauliflower is tender.

4. Add the parsley and finely grate in half the halloumi. Mix well. Check the seasoning and add salt to taste. Divide between four serving bowls and grate over the remaining halloumi. Serve immediately with extra Turkish pepper flakes, if you like.

5 WAYS T͟O DRESS YOUR SALAD

Fun fact about salads: it's all about the dressing. A good dressing will spin a sad bowl of lettuce into something sensational and a bad one has the power to turn even one of Ottolenghi's stunning creations over to the dark side. They should be punchy and tart to the point of wincing, with big flavours knocking your palate for six. But once tossed into your salad, they will temper and mellow. Here are some of my go-to dressings.

01 COOL CLASSIC
This is the classic dressing I was taught when I wanted to be a chef as a teenager and it's often the one that gets the most attention. I think it's best with a green salad. Just whisk up 4 tablespoons of red wine vinegar, 2 tablespoons of olive oil, 2 teaspoons of English mustard, 2 teaspoons of caster sugar and a good pinch of sea salt and pepper.

02 CREAMY COMFORT
This silky-smooth dressing is a killer combo of 60g (2oz) of tahini, 60ml (2fl oz/¼ cup) of water, the juice of half a lemon, plenty of sea salt and pepper and the option of half a clove of crushed garlic. It's amazing with a roasted vegetable salad.

03 TART TANG

Another sharp favourite of mine is a perfumed pomegranate dressing. I love it with chicken salads, root vegetables and grains. Just whisk up 2 tablespoons of pomegranate molasses with the juice of half a lemon, 2 tablespoons of olive oil and a good pinch of sea salt and pepper.

04 HERBY HEAVEN

I adore herby dressings. Why would you not want to salsa up everything in your life? Get a mini chopper or small food processor and blitz up any combo of soft herbs: dill, basil, coriander, parsley or mint are perfect. Blitz two good handfuls of the leaves with half a clove of garlic, 2 tablespoons of white wine vinegar, 2 tablespoons of olive oil, 1 teaspoon of caster sugar and a good pinch of sea salt and pepper. It's amazing with halloumi or warm grains.

05 BANGING BARBECUE

Smoked paprika, one of my storecupboard heroes, is like a little barbecue in a box and great for making grown-up salad dressings. Bash a clove of garlic with some sea salt until you have a paste. Mix in 2 teaspoons of smoked paprika, 1 tablespoon of red wine vinegar, 2 tablespoons of olive oil, 1 tablespoon of water and 1 teaspoon of caster sugar. It's awesome drizzled over potatoes or peppery rocket.

EASY
ENTERTAINING

PORK KEBAB PLATTER [47]

◆

COD AND TAHINI TRAYBAKE [48]

◆

LAMB AND HALLOUMI BURGERS [50]

◆

OKRA, TOMATO AND PRESERVED LEMON STEW [53]

◆

SQUID WITH WHIPPED FETA [55]

◆

ASPARAGUS, FREEKEH AND ROSE HARISSA MASCARPONE [57]

◆

DUKKAH CHICKEN SCHNITZEL [58]

◆

ROASTED SQUASH SALAD [60]

◆

SEABASS AND SPINACH BORANI [63]

◆

CHEESY COURGETTE QUICHE [64]

◆

BAKED CHICKEN RICE [67]

◆

WARM AUBERGINE AND SESAME SALAD [68

◆

5 DIPS FOR DUNKING [70]

HAVING MY DINING TABLE LADEN WITH DISHES
AND MY FAVOURITE PEOPLE SEATED ALL AROUND
ME IS ONE OF LIFE'S GREAT PLEASURES. I LOVE
ENTERTAINING. NOW, I'M FULLY AWARE THAT MANY
OF YOU LIKE THE IDEA OF IT BUT OFTEN FIND THE
EXECUTION LABORIOUS. MY ADVICE: GET 90 PER CENT
DONE BEFOREHAND SO ALL YOU NEED TO DO IS A BIT
OF REHEATING AND GARNISHING. REMEMBER A GOOD
GARNISH CAN MAKE ANYTHING SING.

THE RECIPES IN THIS CHAPTER ARE ALL BIG ON
TASTE AND SMALL ON EFFORT. LOADS OF THE PREP
CAN BE DONE WELL IN ADVANCE SO YOU CAN
CONCENTRATE ON ENJOYING THE MOMENT, RATHER
THAN SLAVING OVER A HOT STOVE.

PORK KEBAB PLATTER

SERVES
4–6

This is my ultimate kebab platter – a feast for everyone to tuck into. The kebabs are served with cooked chips – this might sound bonkers but it's a very Eastern Mediterranean idea – as well as slaw, garlicky yogurt, flatbreads, pickles and chilli sauce. Place everything in the middle of the table so you can all help yourselves and build the perfect kebab.

For the kebabs

- 2 tbsp olive oil, plus extra for greasing
- zest and juice of 1 lemon
- 2 garlic cloves, crushed
- 1 tsp coarsely ground black pepper
- 1 tsp dried mint
- 600g (1lb 5oz) pork shoulder, cut into 2cm (¾in) cubes
- sea salt

For the sides

- 300g (10½oz) oven chips
- 150g (5oz) red cabbage
- 150g (5oz) white cabbage
- 2 large handfuls of coriander (cilantro) leaves
- juice of 1 lemon
- 1 tbsp olive oil
- 250g (9oz/1 cup) Greek yogurt
- 1 garlic clove, crushed

To serve

- flatbreads
- pickles
- lemon wedges
- chilli sauce

Method

1. Preheat the oven to 200°C fan (400°F/gas 8). Brush a roasting tin with a little of the oil, then add the chips Pop them into the oven for 15–20 minutes until golden.

2. Meanwhile, mix the olive oil, lemon zest, half the lemon juice, the garlic, black pepper, dried mint and a pinch of salt in a mixing bowl. Chuck in the pork and mix well. Thread the pork onto eight metal skewers – if you are using wooden skewers, soak them first to stop them burning.

3. Preheat the grill to high. Place the kebabs onto a grill rack and cook for 3–5 minutes on each side until charred, golden and cooked through.

4. Next, make the salad. Mix the red and white cabbages together with the coriander, lemon juice, olive oil and a good pinch of salt in a mixing bowl. To make the garlic yogurt, mix the yogurt with the garlic and a pinch of salt in a little serving bowl.

5. To serve, arrange the kebabs onto a huge serving platter. Squeeze over the remaining lemon juice and season with salt. Add the chips, salad, breads, the bowl with the yogurt, any pickles you like, lemon wedges and chilli sauce.

COD AND TAHINI TRAYBAKE

SERVES
4

I love a traybake when I am having people over. It makes life super-easy. Minimal effort, with maximum effect. The base of this cod traybake is a little paste of crushed garlic, Turkish pepper flakes and dried mint. It's a killer combo that adds an incredible amount of flavour. The tahini sauce really luxes it up at the end.

Ingredients

- 2 garlic cloves
- 2 tsp Turkish pepper flakes, plus extra for garnish
- 1 tsp dried mint
- 3 tbsp olive oil
- 350g (12oz) new potatoes, halved
- 1 large fennel bulb, cut into 8 wedges
- 250g (9oz) cherry tomatoes
- 4 boneless, skinless cod fillets (about 150g/5oz each)
- 50g (1¾oz/scant ¼ cup) tahini
- juice of ½ lemon
- a handful of finely chopped parsley leaves
- 20g (¾oz/2 tbsp) toasted pine nuts
- sea salt

Method

1. Preheat the oven to 200°C fan (400°F/gas 8). Bash the garlic into a paste with a good pinch of salt and then mix with the Turkish pepper flakes, dried mint and olive oil.

2. Put the potatoes and fennel into a roasting tin and pour over half the flavoured oil. Mix well and roast for 20–25 minutes until a little golden and just tender.

3. Rub the remaining oil over the tomatoes and cod. Turn the potatoes so they colour on both sides, place the fish into the roasting dish, scatter over the tomatoes and return to the oven to roast for 12–15 minutes, or until the fish is cooked through and the potatoes are tender.

4. Meanwhile, whisk the tahini together with the lemon juice, 50ml (3 tbsp) of water and a good pinch of salt until lovely and smooth.

5. Drizzle the tahini sauce over the fish and scatter over the parsley and pine nuts. Garnish with a sprinkle of Turkish pepper flakes and serve immediately with all the juices from the pan spooned over the fish.

LAMB AND HALLOUMI BURGERS

SERVES

4

Sometimes when I have people over for dinner, I don't want elegant. I want something delicious and casual that we can all dive into with our hands – and that's the joy of a decent burger. My lamb burgers have a delicious twist: tiny cubes of halloumi mixed into the meat. The squeaky cheese seasons the lamb and melts as it's cooked.

Top Tip

Save time by making the patties the day before you want to eat.

Ingredients

+ 1 red onion, thinly sliced
+ juice of 1 lemon
+ 500g (1lb 2oz) minced (ground) lamb, 15–20% fat
+ 100g (3½oz) halloumi, cut into 5mm (½cm) cubes
+ 2 tsp dried mint
+ 2 tsp Turkish pepper flakes
+ 1 tbsp olive oil
+ 100g (3½oz/generous ⅓ cup) mayonnaise
+ 4 brioche burger buns
+ 1 baby gem (bibb) lettuce, picked
+ sea salt
+ oven chips, to serve

Method

1. Start with the pickled onions. Put the onion into a bowl and add the lemon juice and a good pinch of salt. Mix well and leave, tossing occasionally, to macerate whilst you make the burgers.

2. To make the burgers, chuck the lamb into a bowl and add the halloumi, dried mint, Turkish pepper flakes and a good pinch of salt. Mix really well, then divide into four burgers about 8cm (3in) wide.

3. Heat the oil in a non-stick pan over a medium–high heat and add the burgers. Give them a good squish down with a fish slice. Reduce the heat to medium and cook for 3–4 minutes on each side, or until cooked through. I often find you need to flip them several times to stop them burning during the cooking process. This helps keep them super-juicy, so flip them every couple of minutes to get the perfect finish, as long as they have 6–8 minutes in total to ensure they are cooked all the way through.

4. Spread the mayonnaise generously over the bottom of each burger bun and layer up the lettuce, burgers and onions. Top with the bun lid and serve immediately with your chips.

OKRA, TOMATO AND PRESERVED LEMON STEW

SERVES

4

Flavoured with cumin, ground ginger and preserved lemon, my easy okra stew reminds me of Morocco every time I make it. I love how the incredible scents waft through the kitchen. The trick to stop okra going sticky is to roast it in the oven before adding it into the sauce. This also means the stew cooks quickly as the okra is already golden – an easy win!

Ingredients

- 500g (1lb 2oz) okra (ladies' fingers), cut into 2.5–5cm (1–2in) pieces
- 3 tbsp olive oil
- 1 onion, sliced
- 2 garlic cloves, finely chopped
- ½ preserved lemon, deseeded and finely chopped
- 1 x 400g (14oz) tin of chopped tomatoes
- 1 tbsp sun-dried tomato purée (paste)
- 1 tsp ground cumin
- 1 tsp ground ginger
- 250g (9oz/1⅔ cups) quick-cook polenta
- 20g (¾oz) butter
- 30g (1oz) Parmesan, grated, plus extra for serving
- sea salt and freshly ground black pepper

Method

1. Preheat the oven to 180°C fan (350°F/gas 6). Put the okra into a roasting tin and add 1 tablespoon of the olive oil. Season with salt and pepper and toss together. Roast for 20–25 minutes until tender.

2. Meanwhile, heat the remaining oil in a large saucepan over a medium heat. Add the onion and cook, stirring occasionally, for 6–8 minutes until soft and a little golden. Add the garlic and preserved lemon and cook, stirring occasionally, for 30 seconds until fragrant.

3. Add the chopped tomatoes, sun-dried tomato purée, ground cumin and ginger and a good pinch of salt and pepper. Mix well. Bring to the boil, cover, reduce the heat to low and cook for 10 minutes so that the flavours can marry together.

4. Add the cooked okra to the sauce and mix well. Turn the heat up to medium and cook, without the lid, for 3–4 minutes to thicken the sauce.

5. While the sauce reduces, put the polenta into a non-stick saucepan and add 800ml (28fl oz/3½ cups) of just-boiled water. Cook over a medium heat, stirring continuously for 1–2 minutes to thicken. Add the butter, cheese and a good pinch of salt and pepper. Mix well.

6. Divide the polenta between four serving plates and top with the stew. Grate over plenty of Parmesan and serve immediately.

SQUID <u>WITH</u> WHIPPED FETA

SERVES

4

This is a spin on a very tasty Turkish baked prawn recipe called *karides*.
I have used squid in place of the prawns. I love the flavour and think that
it looks super impressive on the table. The hot squid sinks into a base of
whipped feta that has the most insane salty tang – say hello to your new
favourite dip. It's great with salad and warm bread to mop everything up.

Top Tip

The whipped feta makes a fabulous dip to have
on its own with crisps and raw veggies.

Ingredients

- 50g (1¾oz) feta, crumbled
- 150g (5oz/⅔ cup) Greek yogurt
- 400g (14oz) squid rings
- 1 tbsp olive oil
- 30g (1oz) butter
- 2 garlic cloves, thinly sliced
- 2 tsp Turkish pepper flakes
- juice of ½ lemon
- a small handful of finely chopped parsley leaves
- sea salt

Method

1. Put the feta, Greek yogurt and 1 tablespoon of water into a mini chopper and whizz into a smooth, creamy mixture. Tip onto a serving dish and swirl around with a spoon.

2. Heat a large non-stick frying pan (skillet) over a high heat. Mix the squid with the oil and a pinch of salt in a bowl, then cook in two batches for 2–3 minutes, turning halfway, until cooked through and a little golden.

3. Reduce the heat to medium and put all the squid into the pan. Add the butter and garlic. Mix well and cook for 1–2 minutes, or until the butter has melted.

4. Add the Turkish pepper flakes, lemon juice and a little pinch of salt. Swirl together for 30 seconds so the pepper flakes bleed their ravishing red colour into the butter. Remove from the heat.

5. Arrange the squid on top of the whipped feta and drizzle over the butter from the pan. Scatter over the parsley and serve immediately.

ASPARAGUS, FREEKEH AND ROSE HARISSA MASCARPONE

SERVES
4

This is a full-on vegetarian feast that looks way more fancy than it really is. Grilled asparagus, lemony freekeh and creamy harissa mascarpone all come together for maximum flavour. Freekeh is a nutty wholegrain that has a subtle smoky tone. I use pre-cooked packets that just need a little waking up in a hot pan.

Ingredients

- 500g (1lb 2oz) cooked freekeh from a packet
- 2 tbsp olive oil, plus extra for drizzling
- juice of 1 lemon
- 400g (14oz) asparagus, woody stalks snapped off
- 2 handfuls of finely chopped basil leaves
- 4 spring onions (scallions), finely chopped
- 250g (9oz) mascarpone
- 2 tbsp rose harissa
- sea salt and freshly ground black pepper

Method

1. Heat a non-stick frying pan (skillet) over a high heat. Add the freekeh and mix well to break it up. It's often quite clumpy and hard from the packet. Cook for 1 minute to get heat on the grains and then add 4 tablespoons of water to create some steam. Fry for 1–2 minutes until the water is absorbed. This will wake up the grains and make them lovely and tender. Transfer to a mixing bowl and add 1 tablespoon of the olive oil, half the lemon juice and a good pinch of salt and pepper. Mix well and leave to come to room temperature while you cook the asparagus.

2. Heat a griddle pan over a high heat. Toss the asparagus in the remaining oil and a good pinch of salt. Griddle for 3–4 minutes on each side, or until charred and tender. This will vary depending on the size of the asparagus.

3. Tip the basil and spring onions into the freekeh and mix well. Transfer to a serving dish and top with the asparagus.

4. Mix the mascarpone with the remaining lemon juice, the rose harissa and some salt. It will go quite thick so add 1–2 tablespoons of water to loosen it. You want it to be the consistency of clotted cream, but silky smooth. Dollop onto the asparagus. Drizzle over a little olive oil and serve immediately.

DUKKAH CHICKEN SCHNITZEL

SERVES

4

This is my twist on the brasserie classic and it makes a super-casual dinner for you and your friends. The big ingredient I use is dukkah. This is an Egyptian blend of spices and nuts. I buy a coarse-ground version – you can find this in the supermarket – which adds even more texture to your schnitzel.

Top Tip

Get ahead by breadcrumbing the chicken in the morning and store in the fridge until dinner.

_____

Ingredients

- 2 tbsp dukkah, plus extra for garnish
- 100g (3½oz/1¾ cups) panko breadcrumbs
- 50g (1¾oz/scant ½ cup) plain (all-purpose) flour
- 2 eggs
- 4 chicken breasts
- 4 tbsp groundnut (peanut) oil
- sea salt and freshly ground black pepper

To serve

- rocket (arugula)
- 1 lemon, cut into wedges
- 100g (3½oz/scant ½ cup) mayonnaise

Method

1. Mix the dukkah, breadcrumbs and a good pinch of salt and pepper together in a shallow bowl. Put the flour onto a plate and the whisk the eggs in another shallow bowl.

2. Flatten the chicken by cutting open the fat side of the breasts and then put each breast between two sheets of cling film (plastic wrap). Lay them on a chopping board and lightly whack them with a rolling pin until they are about 8mm (⅜in) thick.

3. Flour both sides of a piece of chicken and pat off any excess. Dunk it into the egg and finally the breadcrumbs, making sure it is completely coated. Repeat with the remaining pieces of chicken.

4. Heat half the oil in a large non-stick frying pan (skillet) over a medium heat and add two of the chicken breasts. If your pan is not big enough, just do one at a time, each with 1 tablespoon of the oil. Cook for 3–4 minutes on each side, or until golden and crispy. Lower the heat a little if they are colouring too quickly. Place on a warm dish and cover. Repeat with the remaining oil and chicken.

5. Serve the chicken with plenty of rocket, lemon wedges, mayonnaise and more dukkah sprinkled over the top.

ROASTED SQUASH SALAD

SERVES

4

This vibrant vegetarian feast makes the most of the soft sweetness of squash, balancing out the flavour with salty olives, tangy pomegranate and fresh mint. It's a doddle to make, so your dinner party can be a breeze. Just serve with a huge green salad and plenty of flatbreads for mopping up the tahini sauce.

Top Tip

Mix any leftovers with cooked grains or pulses for an easy working-from-home lunch.

────────

Ingredients

- 850g (1lb 14oz) squash, peeled and chopped into 2.5cm (1in) chunks
- 2 tbsp olive oil
- 100g (3½oz/generous ⅓ cup) tahini
- juice of 1 lemon
- 80g (3oz/⅔ cup) pitted black olives
- 2 tbsp pomegranate molasses
- A handful of torn mint leaves
- 30g (1oz/¼ cup) pomegranate seeds
- 10g (½ oz/1 tbsp) pine nuts
- sea salt
- green salad and flatbreads, to serve

Method

1. Preheat the oven to 200°C fan (400°F/gas 8). Chuck the squash into a roasting tin and add the olive oil and a good pinch of salt and toss together. Roast for 30–35 minutes until tender.

2. Whisk the tahini with 80ml (2¾fl oz/⅓ cup) of water, the lemon juice and a good pinch of salt. It will split and then come back together into a smooth, creamy sauce.

3. To serve, arrange the squash onto a serving dish and scatter over the olives. Drizzle over some of the tahini sauce and all the pomegranate molasses. Scatter over the mint, pomegranate seeds and pine nuts. Serve immediately with a green salad, plenty of flatbreads and the remaining tahini sauce at the table.

SEABASS AND SPINACH BORANI

SERVES
4

This effortlessly easy dinner starts with a base of *borani,* an Iranian yogurt meze, which melts when you top it with the hot seabass fillets. I finish the fish off with chilli butter, a Turkish technique that adds extra flavour and immediate opulence. You can have everything ready well before you want to eat so all you have to do is cook the fish.

Ingredients

- 500g (1lb 2oz) baby spinach, washed
- 350g (12oz/1⅓ cups) Greek yogurt
- 1 lemon
- 1 garlic clove, crushed
- 2 tsp olive oil
- 4 seabass fillets, skin on (80–100g/3–3½oz each)
- 30g (1oz) butter
- 2 tsp Turkish pepper flakes
- 20g (¾oz/¼ cup) walnuts, bashed into a fine rubble
- A handful of finely chopped dill
- sea salt

Method

1. Heat a non-stick pan over a high heat. Add half the spinach and 1 tablespoon of water and stir-fry for 2–3 minutes until completely wilted. Transfer to a fine sieve and squeeze out the excess water using the back of a spoon. Repeat with the rest of the spinach.

2. Transfer the spinach to a chopping board and roughly chop, then transfer to a mixing bowl. Add the yogurt, the juice of half the lemon, the garlic and a good pinch of salt. Mix well and spread onto a serving platter.

3. Heat a frying pan (skillet) over a medium heat. Brush the oil over the fish and season well. Add to the pan, skin-side down and cook for 3–4 minutes until the skin is crispy. Add the butter to the pan and turn the fish. Cook for 2–3 minutes, basting regularly, until the fish is cooked through. Remove the fish from the pan and place straight onto the spinach borani.

4. Turn the heat off under the pan. Add the Turkish pepper flakes and a pinch of salt and mix well. Drizzle the butter over the fish and scatter over the walnuts and dill. Cut the remaining lemon half into little wedges and serve immediately.

CHEESY COURGETTE QUICHE

SERVES
6–8

This courgette quiche uses the flavours of an elegant Persian frittata called *kuku sabzi*. It's very herb-heavy, flecked with dill, parsley and coriander and finished off with barberries. These little red berries add a pop of colour and a beautiful tart tang. If you can't find them, substitute dried cranberries. They work wonderfully.

Ingredients

- 1 tbsp butter
- 320g (11½ oz) packet of shortcrust pastry
- 2 tbsp olive oil
- 2 courgettes (zucchini), coarsely grated
- 8 spring onions (scallions), roughly chopped
- 2 large handfuls of finely chopped dill
- a large handful of roughly chopped parsley leaves
- a large handful of roughly chopped coriander (cilantro) leaves
- 300ml (10fl oz/1¼ cups) double (heavy) cream
- 3 eggs, whisked
- 180g (6oz) Cheddar, grated
- zest of 1 lemon
- 6g (¼oz) barberries or 20g (¾oz) dried cranberries
- sea salt and freshly ground black pepper
- a large handful of watercress, to serve

Method

1. Preheat the oven to 180°C fan (350°F/gas 6) and butter a 23 x 2.5cm (9 x 1in) loose-bottomed, fluted flan tin. Line the tin with the pastry and trim off the excess. Prick several holes in the bottom with a fork to stop it rising. Scrunch up some baking parchment and place over the pastry. Fill with baking beans or dried pulses and spread them out evenly. Bake for 15 minutes. Remove the baking parchment and beans, then return the pastry case to the oven and bake for another 5 minutes until the pastry is a little golden. Leave for 5 minutes to cool slightly.

2. Meanwhile, heat the oil in a large non-stick frying pan (skillet) over a high heat. Add the courgettes, spring onions and a good pinch of salt. Stir-fry for 5–6 minutes until the moisture has come out of the courgettes and they are starting to fry. Add the herbs and mix well. Stir-fry for 1–2 minutes until wilted.

3. Tip the courgette mixture into a mixing bowl and add the cream, eggs, Cheddar, lemon zest and a good pinch of salt and pepper. Mix together really well, then pour into the pastry case. Scatter the barberries or dried cranberries over the top and bake for 25–30 minutes until just set in the middle. I love a slight wobble. Leave to cool for 5 minutes to help firm up. Remove from the tin, slice and serve with plenty of watercress.

BAKED CHICKEN RICE

SERVES

4

My one-pan baked chicken rice is inspired by the flavours of an Iraqi fish dish called *masgouf*, where grilled fish is spiced with turmeric, black pepper and fenugreek and served with a tomato sauce. My mash-up is a simple traybake using all the same flavours, cooked together so you get lovely crispy bits of rice on the top and then super-soft parts underneath.

Top Tip

Marinate the chicken a day in advance so all you have to do is assemble and cook the traybake.

Ingredients

- 4 garlic cloves, crushed
- 1 tsp ground fenugreek
- 1 tsp ground black pepper
- ½ tsp ground turmeric
- 2 tbsp olive oil
- 2 limes
- 1kg (2lb 4oz) chicken thighs, skin on and bone in
- 250g (9oz/1¼ cups) basmati rice
- 500ml (17fl oz/2 cups) chicken stock
- 2 red onions, quartered
- 100g (3½oz) cherry tomatoes
- A handful of coriander (cilantro) leaves
- Sea salt

Method

1. Preheat the oven to 180°C fan (350°F/gas 6). Mix the garlic, fenugreek, black pepper, turmeric, olive oil, the juice of 1 lime and a good pinch of salt together in a mixing bowl. Add the chicken and toss together so it gets completely coated in all those wicked flavours.

2. Put the rice into a roasting dish (I use a 38 x 25cm/5 x 10in dish) and pour over the stock. Put the chicken, skin-side up, into the dish. I swirl 50ml (3 tbsp) of water into the mixing bowl to get out all the flavours and pour that into the dish as well. Arrange the onions and tomatoes around the chicken. Cover with kitchen foil and bake for 30 minutes. Remove the foil and return to the oven for 25–30 minutes, or until the chicken is golden and cooked through.

3. Season everything with a pinch of salt and scatter over the coriander. Serve immediately with the remaining lime cut into wedges.

WARM AUBERGINE AND SESAME SALAD

SERVES

4

Baharat means spice in Arabic and it's also the name of a wonderfully woody spice mix that I use to flavour the aubergines in this recipe. Grating the tomato to make a dressing is a brilliant tip I picked up in Israel. It gives you a light juice and no skin. The warm aubergines drink this up when you toss everything together.

Ingredients

- 6 tbsp olive oil
- 3 tsp baharat
- 3 large aubergines (eggplants) (400g/14oz each), each cut into 8 wedges
- 2 tomatoes
- 1 garlic clove, crushed
- a large handful of oregano leaves
- juice of ½ lemon
- 250g (9oz/1 cup) Greek yogurt
- 2 tsp toasted sesame seeds
- sea salt and freshly ground black pepper

Method

1. Preheat the oven to 200°C fan (400°F/gas 8). Mix 4 tbsp of olive oil with the baharat and a good pinch of salt. Brush all over the aubergine wedges and pop them into roasting tin. Roast for 30–35 minutes until tender.

2. Meanwhile, grate the tomatoes into a large mixing bowl using the coarse side of a grater. Add the garlic, most of the oregano, the lemon juice, remaining olive oil and a pinch of salt and pepper. Mix well. Add the cooked aubergines to the bowl and toss in the dressing so they are completely coated.

3. Spread the yogurt onto a serving dish. Top with the aubergines and drizzle over the dressing left in the bowl. Scatter over the sesame seeds and remaining oregano and dive on in.

5

DIPS FOR DUNKING

Whenever I have a large group of people over for a meal – with a family like mine, that's at least once a week – I love shoving a load of dips onto the table with flatbreads, crunchy veggies and a bag of Doritos (come on, they are SO good), so everyone can dive in and help themselves. My favourite dips or meze are all super-easy to make and can be done well in advance, so you can have them boxed up and good to go in the fridge well before everyone arrives. All I do is get them out about 30 minutes before serving so they come to room temperature. These will all serve 4–6.

01 TURKISH ÇACIK
This creamy Turkish delight is so refreshing. First, deseed and grate half a cucumber, and squeeze out all the excess moisture. I use my hands over the sink. Pop the cucumber into a bowl and add 300g (10½oz) of the best full-fat yogurt, 2 large handfuls of finely chopped dill, the juice of half a lemon, 1 crushed garlic clove, 3 tablespoons of olive oil and a good pinch of sea salt. Mix everything together and get dunking.

02 SMOKED AUBERGINE MOUTABAL
This luscious Lebanese delight is so sophisticated and so easy to make. Cook 2 aubergines over a gas flame or in the oven (see page 97), then mix the pulped flesh with the juice of 1 lemon, 160g (5½oz) tahini and a good pinch of sea salt. I like to garnish mine with finely chopped mint and a pinch of sumac.

03 **BUTTER BEAN HUMMUS**
This riff on the classic
is so lovely and an interesting
alternative to its chickpea cousin.
Drain a 400g (14oz) tin of butter
beans, reserving the liquid,
then blitz the beans in a food
processor with 100ml (3½fl oz/
scant ½ cup) of the reserved
liquid, 1 garlic clove, the juice
of half a lemon, 1 teaspoon of
ground cumin, 120g (4oz) tahini
and a good pinch of sea salt. If
it's too claggy, add a splash more
of the butter bean liquid. It should
be lovely and smooth.

04 **MUHAMMARA**
This tangy Syrian meze is
off-the-dial good and very quick
to make. Buy a jar of roasted
red peppers. Drain and blitz
6 of them with 2 tablespoons
of pomegranate molasses,
2 tablespoons of olive oil, 2 garlic
cloves, 60g (2oz) walnuts,
2 teaspoons of ground cumin,
4 teaspoons of Turkish pepper
flakes and a good pinch of sea
salt in a food processor until
lovely and smooth.

05 **POMEGRANATE**
AND CHILLI SALSA
Think a Middle Eastern version
of a Mexican salsa. Finely
chop – using a knife or food
processor – half a red onion, half
a deseeded cucumber, half a
red chilli, a handful of chopped
parsley leaves and 2 deseeded
tomatoes. You want a fine
chunk, not a sauce. Mix this with
4 tablespoons of pomegranate
molasses, 2 tablespoons of olive
oil and a good pinch of sea salt.

COMFORT

FOOD

TO ME, COMFORT FOOD IS ABOUT EATING SOMETHING
THAT WILL TAKE THE EDGE OFF LIFE. BY THAT I MEAN
WHEN YOU FEEL STRESSED OUT AFTER A LONG WEEK
AT WORK, SUFFERING FROM A SAVAGE HANGOVER,
HAD A BAD DATE OR, FRANKLY, ANYTIME YOU JUST
NEED A FOOD HUG ON THE SOFA.

COMFORT FOOD CAN BE WHATEVER YOU NEED IT
TO BE. FOR SOME, IT MAY BE A MOUND OF CHIPS
AND MAYONNAISE; FOR OTHERS, THAT CAKE THEIR
MUM USE TO MAKE WHEN THEY WERE LITTLE. FOR
ME, PASTA IS A BIG ONE — I ADORE IT — AS WELL AS
ANYTHING CHEESY OR MY FAVOURITE CHICKEN KEBAB.
I HOPE THESE DISHES BRING YOU AS MUCH JOY AS
THEY DO ME WHEN YOU NEED THEM MOST.

HOT DOGS

SERVES

4

Ever since I was little, I have always adored hot dogs – the more toppings the better. This grown-up version is epic! The hot dogs are loaded with charred red peppers and onions, which have been cooked in plenty of smoked paprika and vinegar, then topped with melted cheese, pickles and yellow mustard.

Ingredients

- 3 tbsp olive oil
- 2 red (bell) peppers, thinly sliced
- 1 red onion, thinly sliced
- 2 tbsp red wine vinegar
- 1 tsp smoked paprika
- 4 smoked frankfurters
- 4 brioche hot dog buns
- 60g (2oz/¼ cup) mayonnaise
- 4 slices of Monterey Jack cheese (about 80g/3oz)
- sea salt

To serve

- 30g (1oz) cornichon pickles, finely chopped
- American yellow mustard

Method

1. Heat 2 tablespoons of the oil in a non-stick frying pan (skillet) over a medium heat. Chuck the peppers and onion into the pan with a good pinch of salt. Mix well and cook, stirring occasionally, for 15–20 minutes until really soft and tender. Add the red wine vinegar, smoked paprika and a little more salt. Mix well so the peppers and onions are completely coated. Turn off the heat and set to one side.

2. Meanwhile, preheat the oven to 200°C fan (400°F/gas 8). Heat the remaining oil in a frying pan and cook the frankfurters for 2–3 minutes each side until warmed through, or as directed on the packet.

3. Cut the hot dog buns open across the top (rather than the side) and pull them open. Slather on the mayonnaise and top each one with a frankfurter. Tear over the cheese so it covers most of the frankfurter. Pop into an ovenproof dish and cook for 5–6 minutes or until the cheese has melted.

4. To serve, top each hot dog with plenty of the pepper and onion mixture and zig-zag over the mustard. Scatter over the cornichons and dive in.

CHORIZO RAGU WITH PAPPARDELLE

SERVES
4

After a long week at work, you can't beat an indulgent bowl of pasta and my Chorizo Ragu with Pappardelle is so easy to make. I use a mixture of regular pork sausages and cooking chorizo, which looks like a regular sausage and needs the same amount of cooking time. If you can't find cooking chorizo use standard smoked chorizo, chopped nice and fine so it runs through the pasta. Simply chuck it into the pan with the onion.

Top Tip

Cook double portions of the sauce. It freezes well for up to 4 weeks.

—————

Ingredients

- 100g (3½oz) chorizo cooking sausage
- 250g (9oz) pork sausages
- 1 red onion, finely chopped
- 2 garlic cloves, finely chopped
- 2 tsp hot smoked paprika (or sweet if you like)
- 1 x 400g (14oz) tin of chopped tomatoes
- 2 tbsp tomato purée (paste)
- 400g (14oz) pappardelle
- A small handful of basil leaves, to serve
- sea salt
- Parmesan, to serve

Method

1. Remove the skins from the chorizo and sausages and break the meat into small pieces.

2. Heat a large non-stick pan over a medium heat and add the chorizo and sausage meat. Spread them out in the pan and leave for a minute to get some heat on them. Cook, stirring regularly, for 8–10 minutes, breaking up the meat as you go, until golden and a little crispy. Remove with a slotted spoon to leave the fat in the pan.

3. Chuck the onion into the pan with the fat and cook, stirring occasionally, for 4–5 minutes until golden. Add the garlic, mix well and cook for 10 seconds until fragrant. Add the paprika, chopped tomatoes, tomato

purée, 200ml (7fl oz/scant 1 cup) of just-boiled water and a good pinch of salt. Return the sausage and chorizo mixture to the pan. Mix well. Cover, reduce the heat to low and cook, stirring occasionally, for 30–35 minutes or until the sausage meat is cooked through and the sauce really rich.

4. Meanwhile, cook the pasta in boiling salted water for 8–10 minutes, or according to the packet instructions, until al dente.

5. Add the pasta to the pan with the sauce and mix well. Cook for 1–2 minutes, mixing continuously, until the ragu clings to the pasta. Check the seasoning and add salt to taste. Serve immediately with basil ripped over the top and plenty of Parmesan.

CHICKEN SHAWARMA

SERVES

4

Chicken shawarma is one of my favourite dishes, but it can be hard to replicate that lip-smacking kebab-shop vibe at home. To nail it, I use a very quick and easy marinade: baharat and garlic provide flavour while yogurt and lemon tenderise the meat. Then I layer up the chicken in a loaf tin. This keeps it super-succulent in the oven. You'll really notice the difference when you dive into your kebab.

Ingredients

- 3 tbsp olive oil
- juice of 1 lemon
- 50g (1¾oz/¼ cup) Greek yogurt
- 4 garlic cloves, crushed
- 2 tsp baharat
- 600g (1lb 5oz) boneless, skinless chicken thigh fillets
- 1 red onion, cut into rings
- 250g (9oz) hummus (see page 135)
- 4 flatbreads
- 1 little gem (bibb) lettuce, shredded
- sea salt
- pickles and chilli sauce, to serve

Method

1. Preheat the oven to 200°C fan (400°F/gas 8). Put 2 tablespoons of the olive oil, the juice of half a lemon, the yogurt, garlic, baharat and a good pinch of salt into a mixing bowl and mix well. Add the chicken and toss in the marinade. Layer the chicken into a 14 x 25cm (10 x 5in) non-stick loaf tin. Put the onion on top and drizzle over the remaining oil. Roast for 30–35 minutes until the chicken is cooked through and tender.

2. Slice the chicken into bite-sized pieces and put in a serving dish. Squeeze over the remaining lemon juice and add some salt. Spoon over a few tablespoons of the cooking juices and toss together.

3. Slather the hummus onto the flatbreads and top with the lettuce, chicken and onions. Serve immediately with pickles and chilli sauce at the table.

ONE-POT MAC AND CHEESE

SERVES

4

This ridiculously easy mac and cheese is a mixture of a gooey, American-style mac and cheese and an Arabic dish called *macarona bil laban*, where the pasta is mixed with very thick yogurt that's almost like cream cheese. Cooking the pasta first in milk gives it a very intense richness and the Monterey Jack cheese creates that perfect cheese pull when you take a forkful.

Top Tip

Add crispy bacon bits or fried onions as an extra garnish if you're feeling fancy.

Ingredients

- 1 litre (34fl oz/4 cups) whole milk
- 400g (14oz/generous 2 cups) fusilli pasta, or a shape you like
- a grating of fresh nutmeg
- 60g (2oz) cream cheese
- 100g (3½oz) Monterey Jack cheese, grated
- 40g (1½oz) butter
- 1½ tsp Turkish pepper flakes, plus extra for sprinkling
- sea salt

Method

1. Pour the milk into a large saucepan and bring to the boil over a medium heat, stirring occasionally. It will take about 6–8 minutes. Keep an eye on it so it doesn't burn.

2. Tip the pasta into the pan with the milk. Add the nutmeg and stir together. Cover, reduce the heat to low and cook, stirring occasionally, for 18–20 minutes, or until the pasta is cooked through.

3. Add the cream cheese and Monterey Jack to the pan with the pasta and season well with salt. Pour in 150–200ml (5–7fl oz/scant ⅔–scant 1 cup) of just-boiled water and mix together until super-creamy. Check the seasoning is perfect. Turn off the heat and leave covered while you cook the butter.

4. Melt the butter in a small pan over a medium heat. Add the Turkish pepper flakes and a pinch of salt. Once bubbling, remove from the heat and swirl together.

5. Divide the pasta between four serving bowls and drizzle over the butter. Serve immediately with extra Turkish pepper flakes if you like.

LOADED FRIES

SERVES

4-6

Perfect for the ultimate Sunday sofa session, this is luxe junk food at its best: beautifully spiced beef spread generously over crispy oven chips and served with plenty of oozy melted cheese, pickled onions and chilli sauce. The spices in the beef give it such an intense flavour; just a little cumin and allspice and you are good to go.

Ingredients

- 600g (1lb 5oz) oven chips
- 2 tbsp olive oil plus extra for greasing
- 400g (14oz) minced (ground) beef, 10–15% fat
- 2 tsp ground cumin
- 1 tsp allspice
- 2 tbsp tomato purée (paste)
- 1 red onion, thinly sliced into half moons
- juice of 1 lemon
- 200g (7oz) mozzarella, grated
- A handful of coriander (cilantro) leaves
- 1 red chilli, deseeded if you like, finely sliced
- sea salt
- sriracha sauce, to serve (optional)

Method

1. Preheat the oven to 200°C fan (400°F/gas 8). Brush a roasting tin with a little oil, then add the chips. Pop the chips into a roasting tin and cook for 20–25 minutes until cooked through and a little golden.

2. Meanwhile, heat the oil in a frying pan (skillet) over a medium heat. Add the beef and spread it around. Leave it for about 2 minutes to really get some heat and colour on it and then stir-fry for 4–5 minutes until cooked through and a little crispy. Add the cumin, allspice, tomato purée, a good pinch of salt and 100ml (3½fl oz/scant ½ cup) of water. Mix well and cook for 1–2 minutes until rich and thick.

3. Meanwhile, put the onion into a bowl. Add the lemon juice and a good pinch of salt. Mix well and leave, tossing occasionally, to macerate for 10 minutes.

4. Arrange the beef over the chips and scatter the cheese over the top. Pop back into the oven for 4–5 minutes until the cheese has melted.

5. Top with coriander, chilli and pickled onions. Zig-zag over the sriracha, if using, and serve immediately.

STICKY POMEGRANATE CHICKEN WINGS

SERVES

4

There is something so satisfying about a beautifully cooked chicken wing. The crispy skin, gooey meat and, let's not forget, a killer sauce. My chicken wings are a total flavour fusion, using tangy pomegranate molasses and ras el hanout. This Moroccan spice mix means 'top of the shop'. The old spice merchants would cream off the best spices to make this famous blend which, by the way, you can grab in the supermarket. You will also notice baking powder in the ingredients. No, this is not a typo. The baking powder performs oven alchemy and makes the chicken skin super-crispy. Clever or what?

Top Tip

This works well with chicken drumsticks – perfect for a picnic. Just cook them a little longer.

Ingredients

- 1 tbsp + 1 tsp ras el hanout
- 1 tsp baking powder
- 1kg (1lb 4oz) chicken wings
- 2 tbsp pomegranate molasses
- 1 tbsp tomato purée (paste)
- 4 tsp light muscovado sugar
- sea salt

Method

1. Preheat the oven to 200°C fan (400°F/gas 8). Mix 1 tablespoon of the ras el hanout with the baking powder and a good pinch of salt in a large mixing bowl. Chuck in the wings and toss well. Transfer to a roasting tin and arrange them skin-side up. Roast for 35–40 minutes until charred and tender.

2. Meanwhile, whisk together the pomegranate molasses, tomato purée, muscovado sugar, remaining ras el hanout and a pinch of salt.

3. Brush the glaze over the wings and return to the oven for 3–5 minutes until sticky. Arrange the wings on a serving dish and serve immediately.

BAKED SWEET POTATOES
WITH GREEN TAHINI

SERVES

4

Despite the addition of bacon, my baked sweet potatoes are inspired by the cool cuisine of Tel Aviv. Here vegetables are the star of the show and often it's the condiments they come with that take them to the next level. The green tahini is everything: rich and delicious, but also spicy and herby at the same time, cutting through the sweetness of the potatoes. That's why I added the bacon. I feel it screams for something salty.

Ingredients

- 2 tbsp olive oil
- 4 sweet potatoes
- 4 rashers of streaky bacon (about 100g/3½oz), finely sliced
- 160g (5½oz) tahini (below)
- 1 red onion, finely sliced
- juice of 1 lemon
- 2 handfuls of roughly chopped parsley leaves
- 2 tsp sumac
- sea salt and freshly ground black pepper

For the green tahini

- 80g (3oz/⅓ cup) tahini
- juice of 1 lemon
- ½ garlic clove
- ½ green chilli, deseeded if you like
- A handful of coriander (cilantro) leaves
- a handful of parley leaves
- sea salt

Method

1. Preheat the oven to 200°C fan (400°F/gas 8). Rub 2 tablespoons of the oil over the sweet potatoes and season well with salt and pepper. Place into a roasting tin and roast for 40–60 minutes, depending on size, until tender.

2. Meanwhile, heat a non-stick frying pan (skillet) over a medium heat and chuck in the bacon. Stir-fry for 4–6 minutes until crispy.

3. To make the green tahini, put all the tahini ingredients into a food processor with 80ml (2¾fl oz/⅓ cup) of water and a good pinch of salt. Blitz until smooth.

4. Put the red onion into a bowl and add the lemon juice and a pinch of salt. Mix well and leave for 5 minutes to allow the onion to mellow. Add the parsley and sumac and mix well.

5. To serve, transfer the potatoes to serving plates and slice them open. Pour over plenty of the tahini sauce and top with the onion salad and bacon. Drizzle over a little more sauce and serve immediately.

GREEN HARISSA GRILLED CHEESE

SERVES

4

There is something so nostalgic about a grilled cheese sarnie. When I was little, my mum used to cook them for us when we got in late after a family holiday – a quick throw-together dinner that feels so indulgent. My version has a good kick with the cheesy filling spiked with green harissa, a North African-inspired paste made from blitzing chilli, fresh herbs, lemon and pickles.

Top Tip
Use the same filling to stuff chicken breasts and roast in the oven.

Ingredients
- 330g (11oz) Monterey Jack cheese, grated
- 160g (5½oz/⅔ cup) mayonnaise
- 1 green chilli, deseeded if you like, finely chopped
- A handful of finely chopped parsley leaves
- A handful of finely chopped coriander (cilantro) leaves
- zest of 1 lemon
- 8 cornichons, finely chopped
- 8 slices sourdough bread
- 30g (1oz) butter
- sea salt

Method
1. Put the Monterey Jack, mayonnaise, chilli, parsley, coriander, lemon zest, cornichons and a good pinch of salt into a mixing bowl and mix together.

2. Spread all the sourdough slices with the butter, then place 4 slices, buttered-side down, onto a chopping board. Divide the cheese mixture among the 4 slices and spread out evenly. Top with the remaining sourdough, making sure the buttered side is on the outside.

3. Heat a non-stick frying pan (skillet) over a medium heat and cook the sandwiches for 1½–2½ minutes on each side until golden and crispy. Depending on the size of your pan, you can cook one or two at a time. Turn off the heat and cover the pan. Leave for a minute so that the cheese goes really oozy. Slice in half and serve immediately.

FRYING-PAN PIZZAS - 4 WAYS

EACH TOPPING MAKES ENOUGH FOR 4 PIZZAS

I developed this method of cooking pizza during that terrible time when London was in lockdown in 2020. I couldn't get to my favourite pizza restaurant, so I recreated that wood-fired effect at home. Starting the pizza off in a searing-hot frying pan gives you more heat than a traditional oven, so the base crisps up quickly. You then pop the pan under a hot grill to cook the top and stop the base from burning. Here are my favourite four pizzas for you to try.

For the pizza base

- 300g (10½oz/2¼ cups) self-raising (self-rising) flour
- 300g (10½oz/1¼ cups) Greek yogurt
- ½ tsp bicarbonate of soda (baking soda)
- sea salt

For the spicy topping (opposite)

- 1 x 400g (14oz) tin of chopped tomatoes
- 200g (7oz) Monterey Jack cheese, grated
- 24 slices of chorizo
- 2 tsp chilli (hot pepper) flakes
- 2 tsp dried oregano

Method

1. To make the base, put the flour into a mixing bowl and add the yogurt, bicarbonate of soda and a good pinch of salt. Bring together into a dough and then tip onto a floured surface. Knead the dough for 4–5 minutes until smooth. Divide into four and roll each piece into a 25cm (10in) circle.

2. Prepare your topping and divide into four portions.

3. Get the grill on high and heat a non-stick frying pan (skillet) over a high heat. Put one pizza base into the pan and spread with the topping you want. For the spicy pizza, strain the tomatoes and spread out over the base. Top with the cheese, chorizo, chilli, oregano and a pinch of salt. Cook the pizza in the pan for 1–2 minutes until the bottom turns golden – lift it up with a fish slice to check – and then put the whole pan under the grill for 2–3 minutes until the

edges are golden and the toppings melted.

4. Repeat with the remaining portions.

Alternative toppings (see overleaf)

• For the meat feast topping, mix the onion, tomatoes, tomato purée, lamb, parsley, Turkish pepper flakes and a good pinch of salt together in a mixing bowl, spread over the pizza base in the hot pan and top with the cheese.

• For the garlic butter topping, mix the butter, garlic and parsley together with a good pinch of salt in a mixing bowl, then spread over the pizza base in the hot pan.

• For the manouche topping, rip the mozzarella over the pizza base in the hot pan. Scatter over the za'atar and a little pinch of salt. Drizzle over the oil.

↘ For the meat feast topping

- ½ red onion, finely chopped
- 2 tomatoes, finely chopped
- 2 tbsp tomato purée (paste)
- 350g (12oz) minced (ground) lamb
- A handful of finely chopped parsley leaves
- 1 tsp Turkish pepper flakes
- 200g (7oz) Cheddar, grated

↑ For the garlic butter topping

- 80g (3oz) butter at room temperature
- 2 garlic cloves, crushed
- A small handful of finely chopped parsley leaves

94

→ For the manouche topping

- ◆ 250g (9oz) mozzarella
- ◆ 2 tbsp za'atar
- ◆ 4 tbsp olive oil

PERSIAN BAKED EGGS

SERVES
4

This is my twist on the classic Persian dish *mirza-ghasemi*, a smoked aubergine dip from Northern Iran. You cook the aubergines whole until super-squidgy, on a gas flame or in the oven, and then add them to a pan with tomatoes, onions, garlic and turmeric. I love taking this to the next level and cooking eggs straight in the smoky sauce. It makes the most indulgent brunch or brinner (that's breakfast for dinner, get it?) any night of the week.

Top Tip

If you're cooking the aubergines over gas, line the hob with tin foil to stop the juices burning.

Ingredients

- 3 aubergines (eggplants), 350g each
- 2 tbsp olive oil
- 1 red onion, finely chopped
- 2 garlic cloves, finely chopped
- 4 tomatoes, finely chopped
- ½ tsp ground turmeric
- 4 eggs
- 50g (1¾oz) feta
- 15g (½oz/2 tbsp) walnuts, bashed to a fine rubble
- A handful of finely chopped dill
- sea salt and freshly ground black pepper
- bread, to serve

Method

1. Prick the aubergines all over with a knife and then place them directly over a gas flame. Cook for about 10–12 minutes, turning every couple of minutes, until evenly charred. You want them to look burnt and a little battered on the outside and be lovely and tender inside.

2. Alternatively preheat the oven to 200°C fan (400°F/gas 8) and roast the aubergines in a roasting dish for an hour until super-soft and tender. Once slightly cooled, peel and discard the burnt aubergine skin. Finely chop the flesh and mash it with the side of the knife.

3. Meanwhile, heat the oil in a large non-stick frying pan. Add the onion and cook, stirring occasionally, for 6–8 minutes until golden. Add the garlic, tomatoes, turmeric and a good pinch of salt and pepper. Mix well and cook, stirring occasionally, for 6–8 minutes until the tomatoes have broken down.

4. Add the aubergines to the pan with the tomatoes and mix well. Check the seasoning and add salt and pepper to taste. Make 4 wells in the mix, crack in the eggs and cook for 5–6 minutes until the whites are set. To help the whites set and keep the yolks runny, muddle the whites into the sauce with a teaspoon every few minutes.

5. Crumble the feta over the finished dish and scatter over the walnuts and dill. Serve immediately with some bread.

ROASTED VEGGIE BURRITOS

SERVES

6

I find these burritos so comforting, with the lovely soft vegetables, rice and sauces all bound up in a crispy tortilla wrap. To nail the veg, cut everything into similar-sized pieces with the onions a little smaller. If you follow this recipe, you'll have more vegetables than you need for four wraps. I always like having leftovers to make burrito bowls the next day. That's everything apart from the bread in a bowl with a little salad. It makes a rocking working-from-home lunch.

Ingredients

- 2 courgettes (zucchini), halved lengthways and cut into 2.5cm (1in) pieces
- 2 red (bell) peppers, cut into 5cm (2in) strips
- 1 red onion, roughly chopped into small pieces
- 1 aubergine (eggplant), cut into 2.5cm (1in) chunks
- 3 tbsp olive oil
- 120g (4oz) basmati rice, rinsed
- 1 tsp baharat
- 1 x 400g (14oz) tin of black beans, drained and rinsed
- 100g (3½oz) tahini
- juice of 1 lemon
- 6 large tortilla wraps
- chilli sauce, to serve
- 120g (4oz) mozzarella, grated
- sea salt and freshly ground black pepper

Method

1. Preheat the oven to 200°C fan (400°F/gas 8). Chuck the courgettes, peppers, onion and aubergine into a large roasting tin so they have lots of room, then drizzle over 2 tablespoons of the oil. Season well with salt and pepper and toss together. Roast for 35–40 minutes, or until golden and beautifully tender.

2. Meanwhile, put the rice and baharat into a saucepan and pour over 240ml (8fl oz/1 cup) of just-boiled water. Bring to the boil over a high heat and then cover, reduce the heat to low and cook for 8–10 minutes, or until the water has been absorbed. Turn off the heat and leave to steam for 5 minutes. Chuck the beans and a good pinch of salt into the pan and mix with a fork.

3. Mix the tahini with the lemon juice, 100ml (3fl oz/½ cup) of water and a good pinch of salt until lovely and smooth.

4. Spread your wraps generously with chilli sauce and then top with rice, vegetables and cheese. Drizzle over a few tablespoons of the tahini sauce and then fold up. I fold the bottom up first and then the sides in to make a pocket. Roll it up, like a cigar, so it's completely sealed.

5. Heat a non-stick frying pan (skillet) over a high heat and brush the base of the pan with the remaining oil. Put the burritos, fold-side down into the pan and cook for 1–1½ minutes until golden and a little crispy. Serve immediately with any remaining sauce drizzled over the top.

5 WAYS TO FLAVOUR A ROAST CHICKEN

I love how the smell of a roast chicken fills the whole house as it's being cooked, the succulent scent inviting everyone to their seat at the table without saying a word. Getting your bird right is easy and I have outlined my method below. But what I love most about a roast chicken is how you can flavour it differently and take it to a new place with minimal effort. Once you've nailed the basic recipe, experiment and serve your roast in different ways. Toss al dente pasta in the chicken juices and serve with the meat sliced up, or try reducing the jus to a sticky consistency and mixing it with mayonnaise to make the base for an epic chicken sarnie.

THE CLASSIC

There are so many ways to get 'the perfect' roast chicken. This is mine. Preheat the oven to 200°C fan (400°F/gas 8) and get your chicken to room temperature. You want a 1.5–2kg (3lb 5oz–4lb 8oz) bird to feed 4–6 people. Rub 50g (2oz) of room temperature butter all over the chicken and season it really well with sea salt and freshly ground black pepper. Place a few cloves of garlic and half a lemon into the cavity.

To cook, slice up 2 onions and pop them into a roasting tin and place the chicken on top. Pour in a glass of white wine and roast for 1½–2 hours, or until the juices run clear. Cover with foil and leave to rest for 10 minutes. The meat will be super-succulent, the skin crispy and you will have a basic jus that you can season and use as it is or make a classic gravy.

01 THE MOROCCAN ONE

Mix 1 tablespoon of ras el hanout and a good pinch of sea salt with 50g (2oz) of room-temperature butter and rub it all over the bird. Stuff the cavity with a few cloves of garlic and a preserved lemon cut in two halves. Cook as per The Classic.

02 THE SPICY ONE

Rub 4 tablespoons of rose harissa over the chicken and season with plenty of sea salt. Cut half an orange into quarters, then pop them into the cavity and cook as per The Classic.

03 THE LEBANESE ONE

Mix 2 tablespoons of za'atar and a good pinch of sea salt together with 2 tablespoons of olive oil. Rub this all over the chicken. Stuff the cavity with a few cloves of garlic and half a lemon. Cook as per The Classic.

04 THE GARLICKY ONE

Mix together 4 tablespoons of Greek yogurt, the juice of half a lemon, 6 cloves of crushed garlic, 2 teaspoons of baharat and a good pinch of sea salt. Rub this all over the chicken. Pop 4 cloves of garlic into the cavity with the remaining lemon half. Cook as per The Classic.

05 THE SMOKY ONE

Mix 50g (2oz) of room-temperature butter with 1 tablespoon of smoked paprika, 2 teaspoons of Turkish pepper flakes and a good pinch of sea salt. Rub all over the chicken. Put half a lemon into the cavity. Cook as per The Classic.

LOW
AND
SLOW

▼

SLOW-COOKED FOOD IS ALWAYS WORTH THE WAIT.
I LOVE HOW CULINARY MAGIC HAPPENS WHEN YOU
THROW A FEW THINGS INTO A POT AND LET IT
LINGER OVER A LOW HEAT. THE FLAVOURS DEVELOP,
INGREDIENTS MELT AND SCRUMPTIOUS SMELLS
FILL THE HOUSE.

MY SLOW-COOKED DISHES ARE ALL EXTREMELY FAST
TO THROW TOGETHER, THE OVEN OR STOVE TOP
DOING ALL THE WORK FOR YOU. MOST ARE READY IN
UNDER AN HOUR SO YOU CAN STILL CONFIDENTLY
MAKE THEM DURING THE WEEK.

LEBANESE CHICKEN TRAYBAKE

SERVES

4

One of the most luscious Lebanese meze is a spicy potato dish called *batata harra*. The potatoes are fried until crispy and then tossed in a garlicky chilli dressing. I have borrowed this element and added it to a chicken and potato traybake. It really does make the most delicious supper to serve any time.

Top Tip
Try using sweet potatoes for a tasty twist on this recipe.

Ingredients

* 600g (1lb 5oz) potatoes, cut into chunky chips
* 4 chicken thighs, skin on and bone in (about 750g/1lb 10oz)
* 2 tbsp groundnut (peanut) oil
* 4 tsp smoked paprika
* 2 handfuls of roughly chopped coriander (cilantro) leaves and stalks
* ½ red chilli, deseeded if you like, roughly chopped
* 1 garlic clove
* juice of ½ lemon
* 2 tbsp olive oil
* sea salt
* green salad and mayonnaise, to serve

Method

1. Preheat the oven to 200°C fan (400°F/gas 8). Put the potatoes and chicken into a mixing bowl and add the groundnut oil, 2 teaspoons of smoked paprika and a really good pinch of salt and mix together. Transfer to a large roasting tin. You want a pretty even layer so things get crispy. Bung into the hot oven and roast for 50–60 minutes, or until the chicken is cooked through and the potatoes are crispy.

2. Meanwhile, put the coriander, chilli, garlic, lemon juice, olive oil, remaining smoked paprika and a pinch of salt into a mini chopper. Add 2 tablespoons of water and blitz into a thick dressing. Spoon into a serving bowl.

3. To serve, transfer the chicken and potatoes to a warm serving dish and drizzle over a little of the dressing. Serve immediately with a green salad, mayonnaise and the remaining dressing at the table.

LAMB TACOS

SERVES

6

My favourite Mexican tacos loaded with Middle Eastern flavours are fusion food at its best – unctuously soft pulled shoulder of lamb, zesty watermelon, salty feta and plenty of yogurt. Put everything into bowls and bung them in the middle of the table family style, so everyone can build their own tacos.

Top Tip

Any leftover lamb is great crisped up in a hot pan and served on top of hummus.

Ingredients

- 1.5kg (3lb 5oz) shoulder of lamb on the bone
- 2 tbsp olive oil
- 300g (10½oz) watermelon, cut into 5mm (¼in) cubes
- juice of 2 limes
- 2 tsp ground cumin
- 150g (5oz/⅔cup) Greek yogurt
- 12 small soft tacos
- 100g (3½oz) feta
- a large handful of coriander (cilantro) leaves
- sea salt and freshly ground black pepper

Method

1. Preheat the oven to 160°C fan (300°F/gas 4) and get the lamb out of the fridge to come to room temperature. Rub the oil over the lamb and season it really well with salt and pepper. Place it into a snug roasting tin and pour 250ml (8½fl oz/1 cup) of water around the meat.

2. Take a piece of baking parchment that will fit over the lamb and wring it out under the cold tap. Place over the meat – this will help keep it super-juicy. Cover the tray with kitchen foil. Place in the oven and roast for 3–3½ hours or until the meat pulls apart at the touch of a fork. Leave to rest for 10 minutes.

3. Meanwhile, put the watermelon into a mixing bowl and add the juice of 1 lime.

4. Take all the fat off the lamb and then pull out the bone. Pick the meat apart with two forks and place onto a serving dish. Add the remaining lime juice, the cumin and a good pinch of salt. Mix well.

5. To serve, put some of the yogurt onto a taco and top with the meat, watermelon, feta and coriander.

MOUNTAIN PORK STEW

SERVES

4

Olives, oregano and orange remind me of my travels around the Mediterranean and these intense flavours are what perfume this pork stew. It's one of those wondrously easy dishes where you chuck everything into a pot and let it idle in the oven for a few hours. I serve mine with giant couscous, which soaks up the sauce sensationally.

Ingredients

- 20g (¾oz) butter
- 1 tbsp olive oil
- 1 onion, roughly chopped
- 6 garlic cloves, roughly chopped
- 800g (1lb 8oz) pork shoulder, cut into 5cm (2in) pieces
- 1 tbsp plain (all-purpose) flour
- 2 tsp ground coriander
- 2 tbsp tomato purée
- 250ml (8½fl oz/1 cup) red wine
- 50g (1¾oz/generous ⅓ cup) pitted black olives
- a large handful of oregano leaves
- zest and juice of ½ orange
- 250g (9oz/1⅓ cups) giant couscous
- sea salt and freshly ground black pepper

Method

1. Preheat the oven to 160°C fan (300°F/gas 4). Melt the butter with the oil in a casserole dish (Dutch oven) over a medium heat and add the onion and garlic. Mix well and cook, stirring occasionally, for 6–8 minutes until a little golden.

2. Meanwhile, put the pork into a bowl and add the flour and a really good pinch of salt and pepper. Toss together.

3. Chuck the pork, ground coriander, tomato purée, red wine and 150ml (5fl oz/scant ⅔ cup) of water into the pan with the onions. Mix well and bring to the boil. Cover, pop into the oven and cook for 1½–2 hours or until the meat is tender. Remove from the oven and add the olives, oregano and orange zest and juice. Mix well. Cover and leave to rest for 5 minutes.

4. Towards the end of the cooking time, boil the couscous in a saucepan of boiling water for 6–8 minutes until tender, or as directed on the packet. Drain and set to one side.

5. Check the seasoning of the stew and add salt to taste. Serve immediately with the couscous.

TURKISH MEAT LOAF

SERVES

4

Tepsi kebab is the Turkish version of meat loaf. The spiced minced meat is cooked in a layer in a shallow dish over hot coals – kebabs can be anything cooked over fire, not just things on skewers. It's an incredible dish. My version is very easy to make and served with a few salads and some bread to mop up the buttery juices. If the thought of fine chopping everything is a mega turn-off, use a food processor to blitz the onion, pepper, garlic and parsley and then add that to the meat.

Ingredients

- 650g (1lb 7oz) minced (ground) lamb, 15–20% fat
- 1 onion, finely chopped
- ½ red (bell) pepper, finely chopped
- 3 garlic cloves, crushed
- a large handful of finely chopped parsley leaves
- 2 tbsp tomato purée (paste)
- 2 tsp ground cumin
- 2 tsp Turkish pepper flakes
- 1 tsp ground black pepper
- 20g (¾oz) butter
- sea salt

To serve

- 1 red onion, thinly sliced
- juice of 1 lemon
- a large handful of parsley leaves
- flatbreads
- 200g (7oz/scant 1 cup) yogurt

Method

1. Preheat the oven to 180°C fan (350°F/gas 6). Chuck the lamb, onion, pepper, garlic, parsley, tomato purée, cumin, Turkish pepper flakes, black pepper and a really good pinch of salt into a mixing bowl and mix together really well. Transfer to a non-stick ovenproof 30cm (12in) frying pan (skillet) and spread out evenly. Dot the butter over the top and roast for 15–20 minutes until cooked through and super-juicy. Drain the juices from the pan into a jug. Pour a little onto the kebab to make sure it stays juicy and season the top with salt.

2. Meanwhile, mix the onion with the lemon juice and a pinch of salt. Mix well and leave, tossing occasionally, to macerate for 10 minutes. Add the parsley and mix well.

3. To serve, slice up the meat loaf and serve with the salad, flatbreads, yogurt and the juices at the table.

BAKED FETA PASTA

SERVES

6

This was a recipe that went viral on social media, filling feeds on TikTok and Instagram. It's super-clever. You bake a whole block of feta with tomatoes and herbs and after it goes super-soft in the oven, you can mash it into a creamy sauce for your pasta. I have added aubergine because it goes gorgeously squishy in the oven and adds an extra veggie hit.

Top Tip

Leftovers microwave well – just add a little water to make the sauce creamy again.

Ingredients

* 1 large aubergine (eggplant), cut into 2.5cm (1in) chunks
* 400g (14oz) cherry tomatoes
* 4 garlic cloves, skin on
* 3 tbsp olive oil
* 2 tsp Turkish pepper flakes, plus extra to serve
* 2 tsp dried oregano
* 1 tsp cumin seeds
* 200g (7oz) feta
* 500g (1lb 2oz) pasta shells
* 2 tbsp sun-dried tomato paste
* juice of ½ lemon
* A handful of finely chopped parsley leaves
* sea salt

Method

1. Heat the oven to 180°C fan (350°F/gas 6). Put the aubergine, tomatoes and garlic into a roasting dish and add the olive oil, Turkish pepper flakes, oregano, cumin and a good pinch of salt. Mix together. Nestle the feta into the middle and flip it a few times so it is coated in the oil. Roast for 40–45 minutes until everything is super-soft.

2. Meanwhile, cook the pasta in a large pan of boiling salted water for 10–12 minutes or until al dente. Scoop out some of the pasta water using a heatproof jug, then drain the pasta.

3. Squeeze the garlic cloves out of their skins and return them to the roasting dish. Add the sun-dried tomato paste and lemon juice and mash everything together until you have a creamy sauce. I like to leave some of the aubergine pieces whole for texture. You need to work quickly here so that the feta is still really hot when you mash it.

4. Chuck the pasta, 100ml (3½fl oz/scant ½ cup) of the pasta water and the parsley into the sauce and toss together until the pasta is super-creamy. Add more pasta water if needed. Divide between six serving bowls and serve immediately with extra pepper flakes.

SPICED SEAFOOD RICE

SERVES
4

When I am travelling around the Middle East, there are certain dishes I can't get enough of and *mujaddara* is one of them. Rice and lentils are cooked together in spices and served with crispy fried onions. I have used this as the base for my recipe and added seafood and peas to make it more of a complete meal. I tend to use a supermarket seafood mixture but feel free to add anything you like.

Ingredients

- 2 tbsp olive oil
- 2 onions, thinly sliced
- 3 garlic cloves, crushed
- 2 tsp baharat, plus extra for serving
- 2 tsp ground cumin
- 150g (5oz/⅔ cup) brown lentils, rinsed
- 650ml (23fl oz/2¾ cups) vegetable or seafood stock
- 150g (5oz/¾ cup) basmati rice, rinsed
- 350g (12oz) mixed seafood (shelled prawns, mussels, scallops, squid rings)
- 60g (2oz/heaped ⅓ cup) frozen peas
- juice of ½ lemon
- A handful of coriander (cilantro) leaves
- 1 red chilli, deseeded if you like, finely chopped
- 150g (5oz/⅔ cup) Greek yogurt
- sea salt

Method

1. Heat the oil in a large, wide casserole over a medium–low heat. Add the onions and a good pinch of salt. Mix well and cook, stirring occasionally, for 18–20 minutes until ridiculously soft and caramelised.

2. Add the garlic, baharat and cumin to the pan with the onions and mix well. Cook for 10 seconds until fragrant. Add the lentils and pour over the stock. Mix together really well. Crank up the heat and bring to the boil. Once bubbling, cover the pan, reduce the heat to low and cook for 20 minutes to soften the lentils.

3. Tip the rice into the pan with the lentils and stir together. Cover and cook for 20–25 minutes until everything is tender and the liquid had been absorbed, adding the seafood and peas for the last 10 minutes to cook through.

4. Squeeze the lemon juice into the pan and mix everything together with a fork. Check the seasoning and add salt to taste.

5. To serve, scatter the coriander and chilli onto the rice and divide between four bowls. Add a dollop of yogurt and pinch of baharat to each one. Grab a fork and tuck in.

KIDNEY BEAN KORMA

SERVES
4

This is a very simple recipe that's inspired by an Afghan kidney bean curry. You cook the beans slowly in a rich tomato sauce with plenty of garlic and spices. I like to finish mine off with a knob of butter. It really lifts the flavour and gives the sauce a silky finish. Delicious.

Top Tip
For a vegan version, swap the butter for coconut cream.

Ingredients

- 2 tbsp olive oil
- 1 onion, finely chopped
- 4 garlic cloves, finely chopped
- 2 tsp ground cumin
- 2 tsp ground coriander
- 2 tsp dried mint
- 1 tsp freshly ground black pepper
- 2 x 400g (14oz) tins of kidney beans, drained and rinsed
- 1 x 400g (14oz) tin of chopped tomatoes
- 2 tbsp tomato purée (paste)
- 350ml (12¼fl oz/1½ cups) vegetable stock
- 20g (¾oz) butter
- a handful of coriander (cilantro) leaves
- boiled rice, to serve

Method

1. Heat the oil in a saucepan over a medium heat. Add the onion and cook, stirring occasionally, for 6–8 minutes until golden. Add the garlic, cumin, ground coriander, mint and black pepper. Mix well and cook for 10 seconds until fragrant.

2. Add the kidney beans, tomatoes, tomato purée and stock to the pan with the onion. Add a good pinch of salt and mix well. Bring to the boil, cover, reduce the heat to low and cook, stirring occasionally, for 30 minutes so the flavours can develop.

3. Remove the lid and increase the heat to medium so you have a gentle bubble and cook, stirring occasionally, for 15–20 minutes until the sauce is really rich and thick.

4. Add the butter and stir together to melt. Check the seasoning and add more salt to taste. Sprinkle with plenty of coriander and serve immediately with rice.

SAFFRON AND PRESERVED LEMON BAKED RISOTTO

SERVES
4

I've always loved saffron risotto. It's both sophisticated and comforting at the same time. My version takes it to the next level. Preserved lemons add even more musty magic to the saffron and I finish it off with cream cheese, an ingredient that brings joy to everything it touches. It's also oven baked, so you don't have to stand and stir for half an hour.

Ingredients

- 30g (1oz) butter
- 1 large onion, finely chopped
- A good pinch of saffron
- 2 garlic cloves, finely chopped
- ½ preserved lemon, deseeded and finely chopped, including the skin and pith
- 250g (9oz/2¼ cups) risotto rice
- 750ml (25fl oz/3 cups) vegetable stock
- juice of ½ lemon
- 50g (1¾oz) cream cheese
- 10g (½oz) Parmesan, grated, plus extra for sprinkling
- sea salt
- chilli oil (optional), to serve

Method

1. Preheat the oven to 180°C fan (350°F/gas 6). Melt the butter in a casserole dish (Dutch oven) over a medium heat and add the onion and a pinch of salt. Cook, stirring occasionally, for 6–8 minutes until soft and a little golden.

2. Meanwhile, put the saffron into a mug and pour over 2 tablespoons of just-boiled water. Give it a mix and leave to infuse for a few minutes.

3. Add the garlic and preserved lemon to the pan with the onion and mix well. Cook, stirring for 10 seconds until fragrant. Tip the rice into the pan and mix well until the grains are completely covered in the butter. Add the saffron and stock and stir together. Pop into the oven and bake for 25–30 minutes until the liquid has been absorbed.

4. Put the lemon juice, cream cheese, Parmesan and a pinch of salt and pepper into the pan with the risotto and mix together really well. I like an oozy risotto, so pour in 50–100ml (3 tbsp) of just-boiled water to get it to the right consistency. Check the seasoning and add more salt to taste.

5. Divide between four serving bowls and serve immediately with extra Parmesan grated over the top and a drizzle of chilli oil, if using.

LEMON AND OLIVE CHICKEN TAGINE

SERVES
4

This is one of my favourite Moroccan recipes, a signature dish you'll find on most menus in Marrakesh. And for good reason: the simple flavours marry together beautifully. I have been a little naughty and added flour to thicken the sauce, which is very untraditional – but hey, I'm British and we love a gravy.

Top Tip
Serve with harissa for extra heat.

Ingredients
* 20g (¾oz) butter
* 1 tbsp olive oil
* 2 onions, sliced
* 600g (1lb 5oz) boneless, skinless chicken thigh fillets
* 1 tbsp + 2 tsp ras el hanout
* 2 tsp plain (all-purpose) flour
* 1 preserved lemon, halved
* 400ml (13fl oz/generous 1½ cups) chicken stock
* 300g (10½oz/heaped 1 cup) couscous
* juice of ½ lemon
* 60g (2oz) green pitted olives, roughly chopped
* A handful of coriander (cilantro) leaves
* sea salt and freshly ground black pepper

Method

1. Melt the butter together with the olive oil in a casserole dish (Dutch oven) over a medium heat. Add the onions and a good pinch of salt and pepper. I like to go heavy on the pepper. Mix well and cook, stirring occasionally, for 10–12 minutes until soft and a little golden.

2. Put the chicken, 1 tablespoon of the ras el hanout, the flour and preserved lemon into the pan and mix well. Pour in the stock and stir together. Bring to the boil, cover, leaving a little gap to help the sauce thicken, reduce the heat to low and cook, stirring occasionally, for 25 minutes. Remove the lid and turn the heat up to medium so there is a steady bubble and cook for 5–10 minutes until the chicken is cooked through and the sauce reduced a little.

3. Meanwhile, put the couscous into a heatproof bowl. Add the remaining ras el hanout and a good pinch of salt and pepper. Mix well. Pour over 350ml (12¼fl oz/1½ cups) of just-boiled water. Cover with cling film (plastic wrap) and leave for 10 minutes. Fluff the couscous with a fork to separate the grains.

4. Add the lemon juice, olives and coriander to the casserole dish and stir together. Serve immediately with the couscous.

PERSIAN PRAWN STEW

SERVES

4

This is a very lazy version of a perfumed Persian stew called *ghalieh mahi*, a spicy tamarind and herb fish stew. To make it more supermarket savvy, I have taken out the tamarind and dried lime – these are two ingredients I adore but they are not so easy to find. The colour of the sauce will fade from a verdant green to dark brown. You can't help it. But I promise you, the flavours develop. It's completely enchanting.

Top Tip

Try cubes of salmon instead of prawns.

Ingredients

- 100g (3½oz) coriander (cilantro) leaves and stalks, roughly chopped
- 25g (¾oz) dill, roughly chopped
- 1 onion, roughly chopped
- 3 garlic cloves
- 1cm (½in) ginger root, peeled
- 1 green chilli, deseeded if you like, roughly chopped
- 4 tomatoes, roughly chopped
- 2 tbsp tomato purée (paste)
- juice of 1½ limes
- 500g (1lb 2oz) raw peeled king prawns
- sea salt
- boiled rice, to serve

Method

1. Start by making the sauce. Save a few coriander leaves for a garnish and chuck the remaining leaves and stalks into a blender. Add the dill, onion, garlic, ginger, chilli, tomatoes, tomato purée, the juice of 1 lime and a good pinch of salt and pepper. Pour in 150ml (5fl oz/scant ⅔ cup) of water and blitz into a smooth green sauce.

2. Tip the sauce into a saucepan and bring to the boil over a medium heat. Cover, reduce the heat to low and cook, stirring occasionally, for 1 hour. This will allow all the flavours marry together and the give the sauce time to get super-rich and thick.

3. Add the prawns to the sauce, mix well and cook without a lid, stirring occasionally, for 3–4 minutes until just cooked through. Add the remaining lime juice. Mix well and check the seasoning, adding salt to taste. Serve immediately with cooked rice and the reserved coriander leaves scattered over the top.

EASY PEASY CHILLI CON CARNE

SERVES
6

This is easy – and I mean super-easy. You throw everything into a casserole dish and chuck it into the oven with some potatoes. Several episodes of your favourite box set later and voila, dinner is served. My chilli has hints of the Middle East: chickpeas instead of kidney beans, allspice for a subtle scent and pomegranate molasses that wakes up all the flavours beautifully and gives it a little tangy tickle.

Top Tip
Get ahead and make the chilli the day before dinner. It will actually intensify the flavour.

Ingredients
- 3 tbsp olive oil
- 1 onion, finely chopped
- 1 red (bell) pepper, finely chopped
- 500g (1lb 2oz) minced (ground) beef, 15–20% fat
- 4 garlic cloves, finely chopped
- 2 tsp smoked paprika
- 2 tsp allspice
- 2 tsp chilli (hot pepper) flakes
- 2 tbsp tomato purée (paste)
- 1 x 400g (14oz) tin of chopped tomatoes
- 400ml (13fl oz/generous 1½ cups) beef stock
- 1 x 400g (14oz) tin of chickpeas (garbanzos), drained and rinsed
- 1 tbsp pomegranate molasses
- 6 jacket potatoes (about 180g/6oz each)
- 200g (7oz) Cheddar, grated
- small handful of coriander (cilantro) leaves
- sea salt

Method
1. Preheat the oven to 180°C fan (350°F/gas 6). Heat 2 tablespoons of the oil in a flameproof casserole dish (Dutch oven) over a medium heat and add the onion and pepper. Cook, stirring occasionally, for 6–8 minutes until golden.

2. Chuck the beef, garlic, smoked paprika, allspice, chilli flakes, tomato purée, chopped tomatoes, stock, chickpeas and a good pinch of salt into the pan. Mix well. Cover and bung in the oven for 1½–2½ hours. This will depend on the size of your pan, but you will know it's ready when the chilli looks dark and rich, and the oils have risen to the surface. Check it every 30 minutes after 1½ hours to make sure it doesn't overcook. Add the pomegranate molasses and mix well. Check the seasoning, adding salt to taste.

3. Meanwhile, prick the potatoes with a fork and rub the remaining oil all over them. Pop into a baking tray (pan) and season with salt. Bake in the oven with the chilli for about 1½–2 hours until golden on the outside and fluffy in the middle.

4. To serve, place the potatoes onto serving plates and cut them open. Top with plenty of chilli and a handful of cheese. Garnish with a little coriander and dive straight in.

5

WAYS
WITH ROAST
VEGETABLES

If like me you're a medium-to-mega glutton, you'll definitely want a big box of roasted vegetables in the fridge so that you can knock up a decent dinner or epic working-from-home lunch in minutes.

My favourite combination is a mix of courgette, red pepper, red onion and aubergine. I love the Mediterranean vibes. Cut the vegetables into similar-sized pieces and chuck them into a roasting tin. Don't overcrowd the tray or they will steam rather than roast. Drizzle loads of olive oil over the top and season with plenty of sea salt and freshly ground black pepper. I also

like a good old pinch of dried oregano, but that's optional. Toss together and roast in a hot oven, 200°C fan (400°F/gas 8), for 35–40 minutes or until golden and tender.

01 VEGGIE WRAP
Lunch on the go doesn't get better than this. Slather a wrap with loads of hummus – frankly you can use any dip you like – and top with the roasted veggies. Add some crunch: this could be iceberg lettuce or a simple chopped salad (red onion, tomato, cucumber and parsley). Don't forget the chilli sauce and then roll up and devour.

02 SIMPLE SOUP
Pour some warm stock over the vegetables; you can use vegetable stock or chicken stock. Bring to the boil, then blitz together. Season with plenty of sea salt and freshly ground black pepper and serve. You could add some coconut milk to make it super-creamy and indulgent.

03 **SPEEDY SALAD**
Mix the roasted veggies with a pack of cooked grains, plenty of chopped herbs and some pomegranate seeds. Season well and dress with olive oil and lemon and you're good to go.

04 **CHEESY OMELETTE**
Reheat the vegetables in a frying pan. Add whisked eggs and plenty of sea salt and freshly ground black pepper. Shake the pan and let the eggs set. I like to run a spatula through them to let the heat in. Scatter over plenty of cheese and fold the omelette in half. Let that sit for a few seconds so the cheese melts, then serve.

05 **PERFECT PASTA**
This is the best dinner after a full-on day at work. Toss the roasted vegetables into some cooked pasta and add your pesto of choice. Season well and mix together. Serve with as much grated Parmesan as you like.

WORKING FROM HOME LUNCHES

▼

THE PANDEMIC RESHAPED ALL OUR LIVES IN SO
MANY WAYS, NOT LEAST, TURNING OUR HOMES INTO
EVERYTHING FROM GYMS TO SCHOOLS AND OFFICES.
THIS CHAPTER IS DEDICATED TO EVERYONE WHO IS
STILL WORKING FROM HOME AND WANTS A DECENT
LUNCH THAT'S READY TO ROCK IN MINUTES.

FROM SALADS TO SOUPS AND CHEESY WRAPS,
I HAVE SO MANY QUICK AND EASY RECIPES HERE TO
TICKLE YOUR TASTE BUDS WITHOUT MAKING YOU
LATE FOR YOUR NEXT ZOOM CALL.

HUMMUS BOWLS

SERVES

2

I am big on hummus; I eat it most days. My recipe is the best way to make hummus with a can of chickpeas. It should be very rich and creamy. The trick is to use the chickpea water from the can to get it super-smooth. Having a huge bowl of hummus is a very Middle Eastern way to eat it. Not a sad tub in sight, just a lemony chopped salad and a soft boiled egg. The perfect lunch that's ready to rock in 15 minutes.

For the salad

- 2 eggs
- 100g (3½ oz) cucumber, deseeded and finely chopped
- ½ small red onion, finely chopped
- 1 tomato, deseeded and finely chopped
- A handful of finely chopped parsley leaves
- juice of ½ lemon
- sea salt

For the hummus

- 1 x 400g (14oz) tin of chickpeas (garbanzos)
- 1 garlic clove
- juice of ½ lemon
- 120g (4oz) tahini

To serve

- olive oil
- 2 pitta breads

Method

1. Boil the eggs for 7 minutes in a pan of boiling water. If your eggs are fridge cold, give them an extra minute to boil. Drain and plunge into cold water to stop them cooking. Drain again, peel and cut in half.

2. Meanwhile, put the cucumber, red onion, tomato and parsley into a bowl. Add the lemon juice and a pinch of salt. Toss together and set to one side.

3. Drain the chickpeas over a bowl so you keep the liquid. Chuck the chickpeas, garlic, lemon, tahini and a good pinch of salt into a food processor. Pour in 100ml (3½ fl oz) of the reserved chickpea water and blitz until smooth and creamy. Add an extra splash of chickpea water if it needs it, about 2 tablespoons should do it.

4. Dollop the hummus into two serving bowls and swirl it around with the back of a spoon. Top each with plenty of salad and an egg. Drizzle over a little olive oil and dive on in with your pittas and a spoon.

TUNA POKÉ

SERVES

2

This is one of those Zen-like dishes that makes you feel fabulous after you've finished eating. It's healthy without meaning to be, packed with plenty of good things: brown rice, radishes, tuna, mango and chilli, and finished off with a kick-ass dressing.

Top Tip

Switch this up with cooked chicken or cooked prawns instead of tuna.

For the dressing

- juice of 2 lemons
- 2 tbsp olive oil
- 2 tbsp maple syrup
- 1 tsp sumac
- sea salt

For the poké bowls

- 240g (8½oz) cooked brown rice
- 4 radishes, thinly sliced
- 100g (3½oz) cucumber, thinly sliced
- 100g (3½oz) mango, cubed
- 1 tsp olive oil
- 200g (7oz) tuna steak
- A small handful of coriander (cilantro) leaves
- 4 tsp pomegranate seeds
- ½ tsp Turkish pepper flakes

Method

1. To make the dressing, whisk together all the ingredients with a pinch of salt in a mixing bowl. Set to one side.

2. Divide the rice between two serving bowls and top each with the radishes, cucumber and mango.

3. Heat a non-stick frying pan (skillet) over a high heat. Rub the oil over the tuna and pan-fry for 30–60 seconds each side until charred on the outside but still pink in the middle. Remove from the pan and slice thinly.

4. To serve, add the tuna to the serving bowls and top with the coriander and pomegranate seeds. Sprinkle the Turkish pepper flakes onto the mango and drizzle over the dressing. Grab a fork and tuck in.

PRESERVED LEMON, PESTO AND HALLOUMI SALAD

SERVES

4

This is a spin on my sister's favourite salad: spinach, pea and pesto. It's very speedy to make. My pesto is classic-ish, but I add a preserved lemon because the fragrance works incredibly well with basil. It's worth making a big batch as firstly, it's delicious and works well with so many dishes; and secondly, it's easier to adjust the flavours in the mini chopper when you have more in there.

Top Tip

Wake up the fried halloumi with a quick blast in the microwave if you're taking this one into the office.

Ingredients

- 1 preserved lemon
- 50g (1¾oz) basil leaves
- 25g (¾oz) Parmesan, finely grated
- 20g (¾oz) toasted pine nuts
- 1 garlic clove
- 4 tbsp olive oil
- juice of ½ lemon
- 330g (11oz) frozen peas
- 200g (7oz) baby spinach, washed
- 250g (9oz) block of halloumi, sliced into 8 pieces
- sea salt and freshly ground black pepper

Method

1. Remove the seeds from the preserved lemon and give it a quick rinse under the tap to wash off some of the salt. Chuck it into a mini chopper and add the basil, about half the Parmesan, the pine nuts, garlic, 2 tablespoons of the olive oil, the lemon juice, a small pinch of salt and pepper and 2 tablespoons of water. Blitz until you have a gorgeously creamy pesto.

2. Blanch the peas for about 2 minutes in a pan of boiling water until heated through. Drain well and chuck into a mixing bowl. Add the spinach. I like to give the spinach a good squish with my hands to break it up a little. I think this helps it to take on more of the flavour of the dressing. Pour in all the pesto, add the remaining cheese and toss together. Check the salt and if it needs a little more, add some here. Divide among four serving plates.

3. Heat the remaining oil in a large non-stick frying pan (skillet) over a medium heat. Add the halloumi and cook for 1–2 minutes on each side until golden and melting. Arrange on the plates of salad and serve immediately.

SMASHED PESTO CANNELLINI BEANS <u>ON</u> TOAST

SERVES
2

Made with storecupboard staples, this quick and easy lunch takes minutes to make. The cannellini beans go really creamy when you mash them, and they soak up all the flavour of the pesto.

Top Tip
The dressed beans make a fantastic picnic salad. Nothing wilts in your Tupperware.

Ingredients
- 1 x 400g (14oz) tin of cannellini beans, drained and rinsed
- 2 tbsp green pesto
- juice of ½ lemon
- 2 slices of sourdough bread
- ½ tsp chilli (hot pepper) flakes (optional)
- 2 handfuls of rocket (arugula)
- sea salt
- olive oil, to serve

Method
1. Pop the cannellini beans into a bowl. Lightly mash with a fork to get a chunky texture. Add the pesto, lemon juice and a little pinch of salt and mix together.

2. Toast the bread and place onto two serving plates. Divide the smashed cannellini beans between the slices of toast. Sprinkle over the chilli flakes, if using, and top with the rocket. Serve immediately with a drizzle of olive oil.

LAZY LENTIL SOUP

SERVES

4

Based on a classic Iranian soup, *adasi*, this dish is perfect for a cosy lunch. It's flavoured with warming ginger, piquant black pepper and mellow turmeric. Although it's very easy to throw together, it's definitely worth making a huge batch.

Top Tip

Batch cook two portions and store one in the freezer for 3–4 weeks.

Ingredients

- 2 tbsp olive oil, plus extra for drizzling
- 2 onions, finely chopped
- 2.5cm (1in) ginger root, peeled and finely chopped
- 2 tsp ground cumin
- 1 tsp ground black pepper
- 1 tsp ground turmeric
- 2 tbsp tomato purée (paste)
- 2 x 400g (14oz) tins of green lentils, drained and rinsed
- 650ml (23fl oz/2¾ cups) vegetable stock
- A handful of finely chopped dill, plus extra for garnish
- juice of ½ lemon
- sea salt
- bread, to serve

Method

1. Heat the oil in a saucepan over a medium heat and add the onions. Cook, stirring occasionally, for 5 minutes, then add the ginger and cook for a further 5–7 minutes, still stirring, until soft, golden and mellow.

2. Add the cumin, black pepper, turmeric, tomato purée and a good pinch of salt to the pan and mix well. Pour in the lentils and stock and mix well. Bring to the boil, cover, reduce the heat to low and cook for 10 minutes.

3. Using a stick blender, give the soup a pulse to break it down a little. I like it with lots of texture.

4. Chuck the dill and lemon juice into the pan and mix well. Check the seasoning and add salt to taste. Serve immediately with a drizzle of olive oil, extra dill on the side and plenty of bread for dunking.

PRAWN, FENNEL AND POMEGRANATE SALAD

SERVES

2

Sometimes you just need a bowl of crunchy green stuff to power you through the day. But you know what, it doesn't have to be boring. Fennel and cucumber are such a great combination. The flavours work beautifully together. I use the side of a cheese grater to get the fennel super-thin because I find it absorbs more of the tangy dressing this way.

Ingredients

- juice of ½ lime
- 1 tbsp olive oil
- 1 tsp sumac
- 1 fennel bulb, very thinly sliced and tops finely chopped
- 100g (3½oz) cucumber, thinly sliced
- 1 orange, peeled and segmented
- 150g (5oz) cooked peeled king prawns
- 1 mild red chilli, deseeded if you like, finely sliced
- A handful of roughly chopped coriander (cilantro) leaves
- 1 tbsp pomegranate molasses
- sea salt

Method

1. Chuck everything except the pomegranate molasses into a mixing bowl. Add a pinch of salt and toss so everything is coated in the oil and lime juice.

2. Divide the salad between two serving plates. Drizzle over the pomegranate molasses and serve immediately.

PALESTINIAN SCRAMBLED EGGS

SERVES
2

In 2019 I went to Gaza, in Palestine, with the World Food Programme, a charity I have supported for years. It was incredible. I was astounded by the food. Noticeably, and unlike the rest of the region, the cuisine is very spicy. Traditionally these eggs are made with a fiery paste of ground green chillies and dill seeds but I have tempered the recipe to make it very easy. The little hit of yogurt at the end makes the dish feel so special.

Ingredients

- 1 tbsp olive oil
- ½ onion, finely chopped
- 1 garlic clove, finely chopped
- 1 green chilli, deseeded and finely chopped
- 1 tomato, finely chopped
- 4 eggs, whisked
- 2 tbsp Greek yogurt
- A handful of finely chopped dill
- sea salt
- 2 slices of toast, to serve

Method

1. Heat the oil in a non-stick frying pan (skillet) over a medium heat. Add the onion and cook, stirring occasionally, for 4–5 minutes until soft and turning golden at the edges.

2. Add the garlic and half the chilli to the pan and mix well. Cook, stirring occasionally, for 10 seconds until fragrant. Add the tomato and a really good pinch of salt and pepper. Cook, stirring occasionally, for 3–4 minutes until the tomatoes start to break down.

3. Pour the eggs into the pan. Season with salt and pepper and mix well. Leave for about a minute and then cook, stirring continuously, for 1–2 minutes until just set. Take the pan off the heat, add the yogurt and most of the dill. Mix well.

4. To serve, put your toast onto two serving plates and top with the eggs. Garnish with the remaining dill and green chilli. Serve immediately.

GREEN GODDESS VEGGIE SALAD

SERVES
2

This is such a brilliant salad that you can knock up in no time.
The green goddess dressing is worthy of the title and more. Fresh herbs
give it its glorious green colour. I like loads of tarragon for its the fresh
flavour. If you're not such a fan, reduce the amount or swap it out for
any soft herbs you like.

Top Tip

Use this sauce as a marinade for chicken
before roasting in the oven.

Ingredients

- a large handful of tarragon leaves
- a large handful of parsley leaves
- 2 spring onions (scallions), roughly chopped
- 1 green chilli, deseeded if you like, roughly chopped
- juice of ½ lemon
- 200g (7oz) Greek yogurt
- 300g leftover roasted vegetables (see page 128)
- 100g (3½oz) cooked chickpeas (garbanzos)
- 30g (1oz/2 tbsp) pomegranate seeds
- 1 tbsp olive oil
- sea salt

Method

1. Chuck the tarragon, parsley, spring onions, chilli, lemon juice and good a pinch of salt into mini chopper and blitz until fine. Add the yogurt and pulse together until you have a light-green creamy sauce. Swirl onto two serving plates.

2. Mix the roasted vegetables with the chickpeas and arrange on top of the yogurt.

3. Scatter the pomegranate seeds over the top and drizzle over the oil. Serve immediately.

ZA'ATAR MUSHROOMS
WITH FETA AND EGG

SERVES

2

Easy on ingredients and big on flavour, this heavenly lunch really reminds me of travelling around Lebanon. Za'atar is such a classic Lebanese ingredient. It's an earthy mix of sour sumac (a tart red berry that's crushed and ground), sesame seeds and dried herbs. It's best mates with cheese, in particular mozzarella or, as in this case, feta.

Ingredients

- 2 eggs
- 1 tbsp olive oil
- 300g (10½oz) chestnut mushrooms, thinly sliced
- ½ tsp chilli (hot pepper) flakes
- 2 slices of toast (I love rye bread for this)
- 40g (1½oz) feta
- 2 tsp za'atar
- sea salt

Method

1. Boil the eggs for 7 minutes in a pan of boiling water. If your eggs are fridge cold, give them an extra minute to boil. Drain and plunge into cold water to stop them cooking. Drain again, peel and cut in half.

2. Meanwhile, heat the oil in a non-stick pan over a medium–high heat. Add the mushrooms, chilli and a good pinch of salt. Leave for 1 minute to get some heat into the mushrooms and then mix well. Cook, stirring occasionally, for 8–10 minutes until tender and a little golden. You want the mushrooms to fry, not steam, so don't move them around too much.

3. Put the toast onto two serving plates and load them with mushrooms. Crumble over the feta. Top each with the egg and season with a little salt. Cut the eggs open so that the yolks start to run, then season with a little salt. Rain down the za'atar and serve immediately.

TIKTOK WRAPS

SERVES
1

This viral food trend makes lunch time luscious again. Think similar vibes to a Mexican quesadilla, except the tortilla is folded to create a pocket that holds the filling. This makes it very easy to eat with your hands and more importantly you can cook several of them together.

Top Tip

Go sweet using sliced banana, Nutella, ripped-up marshmallows and smashed cashew nuts.

Ingredients

- 1 large tortilla wrap
- 3 large, thin slices of chorizo or salami
- 2 spring onions (scallions), finely chopped
- A handful of roughly chopped coriander (cilantro) leaves
- 20g (¾oz) Cheddar, grated
- 1 tbsp red pesto
- pinch of chilli (hot pepper) flakes
- 1 tsp olive oil

Method

1. Place the wrap on a chopping board and make a slit from the middle to the bottom, where six o'clock would be.

2. Dividing the wrap into quarters and filling each quarter with a topping, start with the chorizo or salami in the quarter to the left of the slit you just made, then work clockwise, adding the spring onions and coriander next, then the cheese, and finally the pesto and chilli flakes.

3. Now time to fold. Fold the salami over the greens, then fold that over the cheese and that over the pesto, creating a flavour pocket.

4. Brush a large non-stick pan with a little of the oil and place over a medium heat. Add the wrap, pesto-side down, and brush the top with a little more oil. Cook for 1–2 minutes until crispy, then turn it over. Reduce the heat to low and cook for 2–3 minutes until the cheese has melted and the wrap has gone golden. Place on a serving plate and tuck in.

5 WAYS TO FLAVOUR MAYO

Mayonnaise is the ultimate condiment that can liven up anything from a bowl of chips to a mighty chicken sandwich. It's incredible on its own – as a condiment, not eaten out of the jar with a spoon! But, hey, I wouldn't judge! With a little extra loving, you can luxe up your mayonnaise and take it in a different direction using a few simple ingredients. The following serve 4 in a sandwich or dunking situation.

01 TAHINI
This might sound bonkers, but the mixture of the creamy mayo and silky-smooth tahini is knockout. The mayo mellows the tahini and the tahini enrichens the mayonnaise. What a partnership. Try mixing 2 tablespoons of tahini with 120g (4oz) of mayonnaise. I love this in a chicken sarnie at lunch time.

02 ROSE HARISSA
Combining mayonnaise with my favourite spicy condiment brings me so much joy. Try 120g (4oz) of mayonnaise mixed with 2 tablespoons of rose harissa. It's made for charred vegetables or juicy burgers.

03 **SAFFRON**
This is very indulgent and perfect for a special occasion. Put a pinch of saffron into a bowl and pour over 1 teaspoon of boiling water. This will wake up the king of spice and cause that sunshine colour to bleed out. Mix this with 120g (4oz) of mayonnaise and you are all set. It's incredible with seafood, like juicy prawns or a succulent piece of salmon.

04 **PRESERVED LEMON**
I adore the fragrance of preserved lemons. They work wonderfully with mayonnaise. Deseed a preserved lemon and give it a little squeeze to get out any excess moisture. Finely chop the whole thing, skin and pulp, and mix with 120g (4oz) of mayonnaise. It's best friends with potato salads or grilled lamb.

05 **GARLIC**
My favourite kebab sauce is called *toum*. It's a bright white emulsion of garlic and oil, found in all the best kebab shops in Lebanon. Lovers beware, it's not for the faint hearted. I make a version with mayonnaise that's a bit simpler to throw together. Just crush 2 garlic cloves with 1 teaspoon of sea salt and mix the smooth paste with 120g (4oz) of mayonnaise.

DESSERTS

▽

I OFTEN THINK THAT A CRACKING DESSERT CAN MAKE
A GOOD MEAL EXCEPTIONAL. IT'S AMAZING HOW
MUCH EMPHASIS PEOPLE PUT ON THIS COURSE, AND
IT'S OFTEN REMEMBERED OVER EVERYTHING ELSE.
I UNASHAMEDLY ADORE DESSERTS AND WHEN I HAVE
PEOPLE OVER, I ALWAYS MAKE SURE THAT I HAVE
SOMETHING STELLAR FOR A SWEET TREAT.

MY PALATE IS PRETTY SIMPLE WHEN IT COMES TO
PUDS; CHOCOLATE IS KEY AND THEN AFTER THAT I
LIKE CREAMY THINGS AND A LOVELY TART TANG. SO
THAT'S WHAT YOU'LL FIND HERE: PLENTY OF EASY
CHOCOLATE DISHES, LUSCIOUS VELVETY THINGS
AND A FEW FRUITY BITS AND PIECES.

SALTED TOFFEE ICE CREAM SANDWICHES

SERVES

4

Ice cream sarnies are one of those wonderful desserts that are so easy to make and leave everyone wanting more. Use good shop-bought ice cream and brioche buns, which have a little sweetness that works so well in a pudding. My ice cream sarnies are all about the salted toffee sauce. I like to drizzle a little over the ice cream and then serve each person with their own pot of sauce for dunking. That way there's no arm wrestling over the sauce at the table.

Top Tip

Make the sauce ahead of time and store in the fridge. Just reheat over a low heat in a non-stick pan.

Ingredients

- 70g (2¼oz) butter
- 50g (1¾oz/¼ cup) light brown muscovado sugar
- 150ml (5fl oz/scant ⅔ cup) double cream
- 4 brioche buns, halved
- sea salt
- vanilla ice cream

Method

1. Melt 50g (1¾oz) of the butter together with the sugar in a small non-stick saucepan over a low–medium heat, stirring occasionally, for 3–4 minutes, or until lovely and smooth.

2. Add a good pinch of salt and the double cream to the pan and mix well. Turn the heat up and bring to the boil. Once boiling, cook for 1 minute to thicken. Take if off the heat and give it a good mix together. Leave to cool for a few minutes before serving.

3. While the sauce is cooling, heat a large non-stick frying pan (skillet) over a high heat. Spread the remaining butter onto both halves of the buns and toast them for 30–60 seconds until golden.

4. To serve, put the bottom halves onto serving plates and top each with a few scoops of ice cream. Drizzle over a little sauce and put on the lids. Pour the remaining sauce into four ramekins for dunking and serve immediately.

PINEAPPLE WITH LIME SOUR CREAM AND GINGER SNAPS

SERVES
4

Pineapples remind me of being on holiday. I find the sweet-sour tang utterly alluring. You don't have to do much with them, but I do like giving them a hint of heat to accentuate the sweetness. To make pineapple pop even more, I serve mine with lime sour cream and – wait for it – smashed ginger snap biscuits. The peppery flavour works so well with the fruit and the rubble effect looks awesome.

Top Tip

Cook the pineapple on a BBQ for an extra smoky note.

Ingredients

- 1 pineapple, cored
- 6 tbsp maple syrup
- 200g (7oz/scant 1 cup) sour cream
- zest of 1 lime
- 60g (2oz) ginger snaps, bashed into a fine rubble

Method

1. Cut the pineapple into quarters lengthways and then cut those into long thin strips.

2. Heat a non-stick frying pan (skillet) or griddle pan over a high heat. Cook a few of the pineapple strips for 30–60 seconds on each side until a little charred. Place on a serving platter and brush with the maple syrup. Repeat with the remaining strips.

3. Mix the sour cream with the lime zest and dollop it over the pineapple. Top with the ginger snaps and serve immediately.

LEMON CURD CHEESECAKE

SERVES
8–10

Made with only five ingredients, my Lemon Curd Cheesecake really packs a punch and takes very little effort to make. It's a classic no-bake cheesecake, with a fridge-set biscuit base and cream cheese filling. The flavour comes from your nan's favourite condiment, lemon curd. Remember that one? That sweet, creamy lemony flavour is unbelievable and adds an incredible amount of depth to this dish.

Ingredients

- 200g (7oz) digestive biscuits (Graham crackers)
- 75g (2½oz) butter, melted, plus extra for greasing
- 600g (1lb 5oz) cream cheese
- 180g (6oz/¾ cup) lemon curd
- 100g (3½oz/1½ cups) icing (confectioner's) sugar, sifted

Method

1. Grease and line a 23cm (9in) springform cake tin. Chuck the biscuits into a food processor and blend until fine. Transfer to a mixing bowl and pour over the melted butter. Mix well. Spoon into the cake tin and work the mixture around the base into an even layer. Pat down tightly. Pop into the fridge for 30 minutes to firm up.

2. Put the cream cheese, 150g (5oz) of the lemon curd and the icing sugar into a mixing bowl and mix together until smooth. Spoon over the top of the biscuit base and spread it out evenly with the back of a spoon.

3. Dollop the remining lemon curd over the top of the cheesecake. Try to get about 8–10 little dots. Swirl them around with the handle of a fork to a get a cool pattern and then put the cheesecake into the fridge to chill and set for 4 hours or overnight.

4. To serve, remove the cheesecake from the cake tin and place on a serving plate. Slice into wedges and get stuck in.

FERRERO ROCHER ICE CREAM

SERVES
6–8

I am a huge fan of homemade ice cream and during lockdown I worked on loads of different recipes. As I don't have an ice cream maker, I discovered that the best method was making a base of whipped double cream and condensed milk and then adding flavours. Honestly it is as good as, if not better than, a churned ice cream. It sets perfectly and stays super-creamy. The big kid in me loves Nutella, so I like to swirl in a generous amount and then top each bowl with frozen Ferrero Rocher chocolates. I think the Ambassador would be proud.

Top Tip
Keeps for 2–3 weeks in an air-tight container in the freezer.

Ingredients
- 600ml (20fl oz/2½ cups) double (heavy) cream
- 300ml (10fl oz/1¼ cups) condensed milk
- 200g (7oz/¾ cup) Nutella
- 8 Ferrero Rocher

Method
1. Pour the double cream and condensed milk into a mixing bowl and whisk together using an electric hand mixer until it forms soft peaks when you lift the whisk out of the mixture.

2. Put the Nutella into a mixing bowl and give it a good stir to help loosen it. Dollop 150g (5oz) into the cream mixture and very gently fold it in so that it ripples through rather than mixing completely. Pour into a non-stick loaf tin.

3. Dollop four spoonfuls of the remaining Nutella over the ice cream. Using a butter knife, ripple it across the top. Pop into the freezer for 6–8 hours or overnight to set.

4. Put the Ferrero Rocher chocolates into the freezer with the ice cream to freeze.

5. To serve, give the ice cream a few minutes at room temperature to soften and then scoop into bowls. Carefully cut the Ferrero Rocher in half and place two halves onto each bowl of ice cream. Serve immediately.

CHOOSE LOVE CAKE

MAKES
8-10 Slices

The inspiration for my Choose Love Cake comes from a Persian love cake, a beautifully sticky cake made from almonds, semolina, cardamom and rose water. My cake is much lighter because I use self-raising flour, but it is still packed with those incredible ingredients and then finished off with a generous cream cheese frosting.

Ingredients

* 150g (5oz) soft unsalted butter, plus extra for greasing
* 220g (8oz/1 cup) caster (superfine) sugar
* 3 eggs
* 100g (3½oz/scant ½ cup) Greek yogurt
* 1 tbsp rose water
* 100g (3½oz/scant 1 cup) self-raising (self-rising) flour
* ½ tsp baking powder
* 200g (7oz/2 cups) ground almonds
* seeds from 5 cardamom pods, ground

For the cream cheese frosting

* 180g (6oz) soft unsalted butter
* 120g (4oz/scant 1 cup) icing (confectioner's) sugar, sifted
* 180g (6oz) cream cheese
* 2 tsp rose water
* 25g (¾oz/¼ cup) of pistachios, ground
* 1 tbsp dried rose petals

Method

1. Preheat the oven to 160°C fan (300°F/gas 4) and grease and line a 20cm (8in) springform cake tin.

2. Beat the butter and sugar together until combined, then whisk in the eggs, one at a time, until pale and fluffy. Add the yogurt and rosewater and whisk together.

3. Sift the flour and baking powder into the bowl and add the ground almonds and ground cardamom seeds. Fold together.

4. Tip the mixture into the cake tin and bake for 30–35 minutes until the cake is a little golden on top and a skewer comes out clean from the middle. Leave to cool completely.

5. To make the cream cheese frosting, beat the butter and icing sugar together until smooth using an electric hand mixer. Fold in the cream cheese and rose water by hand until lovely and smooth.

6. Spread the frosting all over the cake and then garnish with pistachios and rose petals. Slice and serve.

PEANUT BUTTER CHOCOLATE TRUFFLES

MAKES
20–22

Need a speedy sweet treat? I've got you covered with my Peanut Butter Chocolate Truffles. The secret ingredient is dates. They have the most amazing caramel flavour and sticky texture that sets perfectly to make a truffle. I like to roll these in smashed pistachios, which gives a vibrant colour and beautiful crunch. If you're feeling swanky, try adding some ground freeze-dried raspberries as well. The contrast of the red and green is amazing. You'll find them in the baking aisle of most supermarkets.

Ingredients

- 300g (10½oz/1¾ cups) medjool dates, pitted and any stalks removed
- 120g (4oz/½ cup) smooth peanut butter
- 180g (6oz) dark chocolate with 70% cocoa solids
- 20g (¾oz/2 tbsp) pistachios, smashed into a fine rubble
- sea salt

Method

1. Chuck the dates into a food processor. Add the peanut butter and a pinch of salt and blitz until smooth. Roll the date mixture into 20–22 little balls and pop them onto a plate. Put them in the freezer for 20 minutes to set.

2. Melt the chocolate in a heatproof bowl set over a pan of simmering water.

3. Line a plate with greaseproof (waxed) paper. Dip one of the date balls into the chocolate until completely coated, then pop onto the prepared plate. Sprinkle over some of the pistachios and a little salt. Repeat with the remaining date balls.

4. Put the truffles into the fridge for 20 minutes to firm up. You can serve them fridge cold or at room temperature, which is my favourite – in which case just leave them out for 5 minutes before serving.

RASPBERRY AND ROSE WATER BAKED OATS

SERVES
4

I must confess, baked oats are not my invention. They were a huge trend on TikTok when I was writing this book. They are made using ground oats instead of flour to make a gooey little cake, similar to a fondant, and they are very easy to prepare; everything is chucked into a food processor to make a batter and then poured into ramekins to bake. I like to have them cooked at the edge and gooey in the centre. You can add any flavour you like to the basic recipe, but I favour rose water and a dollop of raspberry jam.

Top Tip

Make the same base (step 1), without the rose water and stir in plenty of chocolate chips instead.

Ingredients

* 1 tbsp butter
* 120g (4oz/1¼ cups) rolled oats
* 1 tsp baking powder
* 4 tbsp whole milk
* 2 eggs
* 2 tbsp maple syrup
* 1 tsp rose water
* 4 tbsp raspberry jam
* 8 raspberries

Method

1. Preheat the oven to 180°C fan (350°F/gas 6) and butter four 150ml (5fl oz/scant ⅔ cup) ovenproof ramekins. Put the oats into a food processor and blitz for a minute or so until fine. Add the baking powder, milk, eggs, maple syrup and rose water and mix into a creamy batter.

2. Divide half the batter between the four ramekins. Add 1 tablespoon of raspberry jam into the middle of each and then pour over the rest of the batter. Pop two raspberries into the middle of each oat pot and bake for 10–12 minutes, or until a skewer comes out just clean at the sides, with the middle still gooey. Serve immediately.

CHOCOLATE AND TAHINI ROCKY ROAD

SERVES
6–8

This recipe is based on a Turkish dish called mosaic cake, named in reference to the beautiful pattern you can see when you cut into it. Think chocolate and biscuit fridge cake, although my version is a bit more grown up with bitter dark chocolate, plenty of nuts, dried cranberries and a ravishing ripple of tahini at the end.

Ingredients

- 300g (10½oz) dark chocolate with 70% cocoa solids, broken into squares
- 150g (5oz) butter, cubed
- 4 tbsp golden (light corn) syrup
- 150g (5oz) digestive biscuits (Graham crackers)
- 100g (3½oz/1 cup) nuts – I use a mix of unsalted shelled pistachios, pecans and cashews
- 75g (2½oz/⅔ cup) sweetened dried cranberries
- 2 tbsp tahini

Method

1. Melt the chocolate with the butter and syrup in a heatproof bowl set over a simmering pan of water. Line a 23cm (9in) square baking tin.

2. Meanwhile, blitz the digestives into a course rubble in a food processor and tip them into a mixing bowl.

3. Roughly chop the nuts and add them to the bowl, then add the cranberries. Mix together.

4. Pour two-thirds of the chocolate into the mixing bowl with the biscuits and mix well to combine. Transfer to the lined tin. Even the mixture out and press it down gently with the back of a spoon.

5. Pour the remaining chocolate over the top of the rocky road and spread it evenly. Drizzle over the tahini. Using a skewer, swirl the tahini into the chocolate. Pop the whole thing into the fridge for 2½–3 hours to firm up. Remove from the tin and cut into 12 squares. Pile them onto a plate and dive in.

FROZEN BANANA AND DARK CHOCOLATE POTS

SERVES

4

Frozen banana 'ice cream' is a clever hack. Just freeze chopped-up pieces of banana, then blend them until creamy. Now, when you freeze banana, ideally freeze the chunks in a layer on a tray so they don't stick together. I am very lazy and never do this, preferring to bung them into a freezer bag, so I need to give them a good whack with a rolling pin to break them up. Once creamy and smooth from the blender, I serve the ice cream in glasses, covered in a layer of chocolate. It's so satisfying cracking through the chocolate and diving into the soft-set banana ice cream.

Top Tip

Add the frozen banana pieces to a smoothie to give a creamy texture.

Ingredients

- 600g (1lb 5oz) peeled bananas
- 60g (2oz) dark chocolate with 70% cocoa solids, broken into pieces
- 120g (4oz/½ cup) smooth peanut butter
- sea salt

Method

1. This bit you have to prep ahead. Peel and roughly chop the bananas into small pieces. Pop them onto a lined baking tray (pan) and into the freezer to freeze for 3–4 hours or overnight.

2. Melt the dark chocolate in a heatproof bowl set over a pan of simmering water.

3. Put the frozen banana and peanut butter into a food processor and blend until smooth and creamy. If nothing happens, just leave the pieces in there for a few minutes to soften. You might need to move everything around with a spoon a few times to help it catch. Divide among four serving glasses and smooth them out into an even layer with a spoon.

4. Pour the chocolate over the ice cream and swirl around into an even layer. Place them into the freezer for 5 minutes to set the chocolate and then serve immediately with some sea salt scattered over the top.

STICKY HONEY PEACHES

SERVES

4

As you can see from the recipe, this dessert requires minimal effort to throw together but looks incredibly elegant. The peaches soak up the flavour of the butter and thyme, which then makes a thick, drizzly sauce. The rose water cream adds the perfect sweet perfume to finish off your pudding.

Ingredients

- 150ml (5fl oz/scant ⅔ cup) double (heavy) cream
- 1 tsp rose water
- 30g (1oz) butter
- 1 sprig of thyme
- 4 peaches, halved and pitted
- 4 tbsp clear honey
- ¼ tsp ground cinnamon

Method

1. Pour the cream and rose water into a mixing bowl and whisk until it forms soft peaks when you lift out the whisk.

2. Melt the butter along with the thyme in a large non-stick frying pan (skillet) over a medium heat and cook until the butter melts. Add the peaches, cut-side down, and cook for 4–5 minutes until golden and the butter is browned. Remove from the heat and divide between four serving plates.

3. Take the thyme out of the pan and drizzle in the honey. Add the cinnamon and mix well until you have a lovely sticky sauce. Drizzle generously over the peaches and serve immediately with the cream.

5

WAYS TO PIMP YOUR ICE CREAM

Whether you make it yourself or buy it in a tub, ice cream is one of the greatest things to have stashed in the freezer. It's the perfect pairing for a Netflix binge or a delectable dessert after dinner. In my mind, ice cream is a vehicle for the toppings – and lashings of them. Go big or go home, I say. Here are some of my favourite ways to pimp your ice cream.

01 SUNDAE SESH
Drizzle your ice cream with plenty of hot chocolate sauce and smashed nuts or, if you're feeling wicked, some crumbled brownies. I like to make a quick sauce for two by melting 35g (1¼oz) of butter together with 2 teaspoons of cocoa (unsweetened chocolate) powder and a pinch of sea salt. Drizzle in 2 tablespoons of clear honey, mix together and get pouring.

02 FEELING FRUITY
An easy win, which for some reason also feels much lighter, is a fruity sauce for your ice cream. Simply warm up any jam you like so it's drizzly – that killer combo of hot sauce and cold ice cream is everything. I also love the sharp tang of lemon curd swirled over sweet vanilla or strawberry ice cream.

03 DECONSTRUCTED DECADENCE

You can re-set ice cream into ice-cream bombs or cakes, essentially melting your favourite flavour just until stirable and then scooping it into a pudding bowl or loaf tin. You can add anything from slices of cake to juicy berries and pieces of chocolate bars to give them the wow factor.

04 SEXY SARNIES

Why not try sandwiching a few scoops of ice cream between two chocolate chip cookies or a decadent doughnut? It's such a showstopper. Another winner is a toasted brioche bun – they have a slight sweetness that works so well with ice cream (see page 161).

05 COOL CANDY

When I was younger, the ice cream bar at my local pizza joint was all the rage. You could have as much ice cream as you wanted and add any amount of smashed Maltesers, chocolate buttons, Gummie Bears or hundreds and thousands. You never really grow out of something that profound, so give it a whirl. Put all the above into bowls so everyone can trick out their ice cream as they like.

DINNER PARTY COMBOS

If you're looking to feed a crowd and want to pull out all the stops whilst keeping cool in the kitchen, here are some of my favourite recipe combinations. I've included instructions so you can get them done a few hours ahead of time. Always remember, if you're reheating things, check the seasoning and add more salt and pepper to taste.

BANGING BRUNCH WITH MATES

Serves 4

- Veggie Shakshuka (page 27)
- Hummus Bowls (page 135)
- Frozen Banana and Dark Chocolate Pots (page 176)

Brunching with mates? This one's for you. Get the banana pieces in the freezer the day before brunch. On the day, blitz the bananas and pop them into glasses. Pour over the chocolate and put them into the freezer to set. Get the shakshuka cooked, leaving out the eggs. Cover and leave. Prep the hummus bowls, leaving out the eggs and put them on the table. Once you've served mimosas (obvs), re-heat the shakshuka, adding a little water if it looks too dry. Once hot, add the eggs and cook as the recipe instructs. Serve with the hummus and loads of bread. Give the Frozen Banana and Dark Chocolate Pots 5 minutes at room temperature to soften before eating.

MID-WEEK DINNER WITH FRIENDS

Serves 4

- 2 x Steak Tagliata with Zhoug (page 16)
- Creamy Harissa Gnocchi (page 33)
- Salted Toffee Ice Cream Sandwiches (page 161)

If you decide to have company during the week, this one's for you. Remember, you'll need to double the volume of ingredients for the Steak Tagliata with Zhoug to serve 4. Start by getting the zhoug whizzed up and the salted toffee sauce cooked as soon as you get back from work. Then prepare the gnocchi and leave it covered in the pan. When you're ready to eat, cook the steaks and reheat the gnocchi in the pan with a little hot water to get the sauce super creamy again. Serve the steaks with salad and zhoug and the gnocchi at the table. Re-heat the toffee sauce and cook off the buns for the ice cream when you want dessert.

DO-AHEAD DINING

Serves 4

- Charred Dukkah Lamb Cutlets (page 36)
- Cauliflower Rice Pilaf (page 38)
- Ferrero Rocher Ice Cream (page 167)

If you want to be uber efficient, this is awesome as you can prep most of it the day before. The day before, make the ice cream and pop it into the freezer. Get the lamb coated in the spices and the salad chopped. Mix the minty yogurt. Cook the Cauliflower Rice Pilaf, leaving it a little al dente. Box everything up once cool and pop it into the fridge. On the day, get the lamb, salad and pilaf out of the fridge 20 minutes before dinner. Cook the lamb and dress the salad. Re-heat the pilaf in a hot pan with a little water or give it a blast in the microwave. Serve everything at the table, and remember to give the ice cream a few minutes to soften before serving.

ROMANTIC DINNER

Serves 2

- ½ x Pork Chops and Butterbean Mash (page 24)
- ½ x Preserved Lemon, Pesto and Halloumi Salad (page 139)
- ½ x Pineapple with Lime Sour Cream and Ginger Snaps (page 162)

This is a perfect menu if you want to impress someone. It serves 4 but can easily be halved to serve 2. Start by getting the pork marinated. Next, cook the butterbean mash and leave it covered in the pan. Cut the pineapple. If you don't mind dessert at room temperature, cook off the pineapple ahead of time and just garnish it when you fancy dessert. If you want it warm, cook it when you are ready. Prep the Preserved Lemon, Pesto and Halloumi Salad completely. To make life easy, I leave out the halloumi – the salad is just as tasty without it. When you want to eat, cook the pork and reheat the mash, adding a little hot water to get it super creamy again. Finally, cook the pineapple if you haven't already and garnish it before eating.

OVEN EASY

Serves 4

- Lebanese Chicken Traybake (page 107)
- Green Goddess Veggie Salad (page 149)
- Raspberry and Rose Water Baked Oats (page 173)

This is a good one, as you can get everything ready and let the oven do all the work. Get the Lebanese Chicken Traybake ready to go into the oven, then make the sauce. Cover it and store it at room temperature. Put all the veggies into a roasting tray for the salad and make the Green Goddess sauce. Pop the sauce into the fridge. Get the baked oats ready in their pots. Pop the trays of chicken and vegetables into the oven to cook about an hour before you want to eat. They might take longer than the recipes indicate. To serve, assemble the Green Goddess Salad and serve the traybake with the sauce you made. Pop the oats into the oven 12 minutes before you want to eat.

VEGGIE FEAST FOR EIGHT

Serves 8

- Cheesy Courgette Quiche (page 64)
- Roasted Squash Salad (page 60)
- Asparagus, Freekeh and Rose Harissa Mascarpone (page 57)
- Lemon Curd Cheesecake (page 164)

I like to serve the salads at room temperature for this dinner so I can get them done well in advance. Start with the cheesecake and let it set in the fridge – you can do this the day before. On the day, get the quiche prepped up to the point of cooking it in the oven. Pop it into the fridge and crack on with the salads. For the Roasted Squash Salad, cook the squash. Cover the tray with foil and leave it to one side. Mix the tahini sauce, cover and leave it at room temperature. For the Asparagus, Freekeh and Rose Harissa Mascarpone, mix up the freekeh salad and cook the asparagus. Pop them onto a serving plate. Mix up the mascarpone and harissa. Store both in the fridge. Forty minutes before you want to eat, get the oven on and cook the quiche. Whilst the quiche is cooking, finish off the squash salad and plate up the Asparagus, Freekeh and Rose Harissa Mascarpone. That's it you're good to go. Just portion out the cheesecake when you're ready.

INDEX

ACKNOWLEDGEMENTS

Writing a book takes a huge amount of effort from so many people and for *Fast Feasts* the effort put in, under such bonkers circumstances was extraordinary. We had to navigate creative meetings over Skype and work around Covid on set. Everyone went above and beyond to make something that is so beautiful and I am eternally grateful to all involved.

I want to thank Welbeck for taking me on. They are a new publisher for me and I'm so excited to be part of their cooking catalogue. The real hero is my Publisher, Kate Pollard, who saw the potential in me. She is a joy to work with. It's been effortless and hilarious all at once darls.

Getting a cookbook to look bookshelf ready takes a full team and I am very lucky that I work with the best. Sharp shooting on the camera, making each photo look so vibrant is Nassima Rothacker. Nassima thank you so much. Can we go on more far-flung adventures soon? On the food, it's Rosie Reynolds, food stylist extraordinaire and the funniest person around. Lauren Miller stepped in at the last minute to do the proppping and smashed it, getting us a treasure trove of goodies to style each image. And finally, Julia Murray weaved her magic and brought every page to life. Guys we did it. Thank you.

I have been working with my agents at Yellow Poppy Media for many years now – Anna, Geraldine and Kate. They have always pushed me to do great things and believe in all of my mad ideas (well, most of them). Thanks guys. Here's to many more.

I could not have done this without the support of my family. My mum and dad, Sal and Al, are the coolest people I know. Always there when I need them – as long as they are not out partying – and more recently, letting me crash their house to film my recipe videos each week. My amazing mum works with me, fimling and directing everything. I love you both to bits. What special people you are. My sister, Rosie, scooped me up during the pandemic, along with Giles, Daisy, Jake and Dylan, when I needed it the most. What could have been one of the hardest moments in time was made super special. I got to be with you and soak up all your love. My brother Tom, and his gorgeous family, Rachel, Finn and Anya, are always there when I need a distraction and some serious Lego time. Plus, my wonderful extended family – too many to list, but you know who you are. I don't think that you guys realise quite how much you mean to me. You are everything. And lastly, almost family, our Vic Bonny. You have helped me more than you will ever know. Come home soon. I miss you!

Finally, you guys. This was only possible because of the support I get from each and every one of you. Thanks for sticking with me for the last ten years and for pivoting with me during Covid. This one's for you.

Cheers x JGS

ABOUT THE AUTHOR

John Gregory-Smith is a chef, presenter and best-selling author who specialises in Middle Eastern and North African cuisine. He has written six cookbooks, including *Saffron in the Souks*, *Orange Blossom and Honey* and *Turkish Delights*. John is a TV presenter who appears regularly on C4's *Sunday Brunch* and ITV's *This Morning*. He has a Saturday Supper Club column in the *Telegraph*. His Instagram channel has over 80K followers and TikTok 60k, who lap up his everyday easy recipes, all with his signature Middle Eastern twist.

@JOHNGS

@JOHNGS

Published in 2022 by OH Editions
Part of Welbeck Publishing Group.
Based in London and Sydney.
www.welbeckpublishing.com

A CIP catalogue record for this book is available from the British Library.

ISBN 978-1-91431-717-0

Publisher: Kate Pollard
Editor: Wendy Hobson
Designer: Julia Murray
Food stylist: Rosie Reynolds
Prop stylist: Lauren Miller
Indexer: Cathy Heath
Colour reproduction: P2D
Production controller: Arlene Alexander

Printed and bound in China

FSC
www.fsc.org
MIX
Paper from
responsible sources
FSC® C020056

10 9 8 7 6 5 4 3 2 1